Journey
— to the —
Beloved

Journey
— to the —
Beloved

Your Soul as Teacher, Healer,
Guide, Lover, and Friend

Susan Vaughn

New World Library
Novato, California

New World Library
14 Pamaron Way
Novato, California 94949
© 1996 Susan Vaughn
Cover design: Nita Ybarra
Text design: Aaron Kenedi
Editorial: Marc Allen

Library of Congress Cataloging-in-Publication Data
Vaughn, Susan, 1951 -
Journey to the beloved : your soul as teacher, healer, guide,
lover, and friend

p.   cm
ISBN 1-880032-76-7 (alk. paper)
1. Spiritual life. 2. Soul. 3. Meditation. 4. Visualization.
5. Love--Religious aspects. 6. Spiritual healing.
7. Vaughn, Susan, 1951- . I. Title
BL624.V387   1996
248.4--dc20   CIP

First printing, July 1996
Printed in the U.S.A. on acid-free paper
Distributed to the trade by Publishers Group West

To my children,
Nathan, Kalendy, and Katie Rose,
who gave me the time and
space I needed to write this book.

Contents

I searched, I prayed
    for a love that would not fade
Where is true love
    that will never part?

The answer came
    In my darkest, brightest hour
My love was always within
    my own heart

— Marc Allen

Introduction

One night I went to bed feeling utterly depressed. My relationship of ten years was disintegrating. I had a two-year-old, a three-year-old, and a five-year-old. I lived way out in the country in the middle of nowhere in a hand-built house that was only partially completed. It was a long way from being comfortable.

I kept asking myself over and over again, "What am I going to do?" I had no religion to comfort me, no faith, no God, no love. I had never been taught such things and had never even understood what spirituality meant. I was thirty-five years old, had virtually never been inside a church, and had no concept whatsoever of a reality that might exist beyond my five senses.

That night I said the first prayer of my entire life. It was very simple. I said, "If you are there, God, you must send me a guide because I don't know how to find you." Then, because I had no definition of God, I let the prayer go and didn't think about it anymore. Although I wasn't to know it for a long time, it was that night that my journey to the Beloved began.

In those days, I was filled with inner pain. Not only was my dream of a safe and secure home where I could raise my children in peace and harmony a shambles, I had other problems as well. The lifelong allergies I had always suffered from had turned into environmental allergies and I literally believed that everything in my environment, from common foods and pollens to formaldehyde and detergent, was trying to kill me. As a result, I was coughing, sneezing, and wheezing my way through life.

If that wasn't bad enough, I also had rheumatoid arthritis, which I had begun to experience in my early twenties. My nights were a nightmare of tossing and turning as I tried to deal with the pain in my joints. My body hurt everywhere. There was not one inch of me that was free of pain, and every breath I took into my suffocated lungs reminded me of how much I hurt.

Yet the external pain I felt was nothing compared to my inner pain, for I believed that not one soul in the entire universe loved me. That was because I didn't think I was worth loving. Of this I was certain. Although I didn't have a name for it then, I was utterly and completely wrapped in shame. I lived and breathed it. It was all I knew from the beginning to the ending of each day. My external pain was but a dim reflection of the inner pain I carried with me and, like a club, I beat myself up with it every day of my life. The fact that I had never done anything to be ashamed of didn't make any difference. I knew I had created the terrible mess my life was in and that no one was to blame for it but me. No matter how hard I tried, I just couldn't seem to do my life right.

This was the state of my life when my Beloved first came to me as an angelic though unseen being (for lack of a better word) in the middle of the night nearly a year and a half after I said my first prayer.

Though I could not see or hear him because he had no form, he did have a presence that literally filled the room where I was sleeping. In a holy instant of indescribable bliss, I was awakened and he communicated to me, without words, the depth of his love. Although I was ignorant of the spiritual journey at the time, in that instant of deep communion I was changed forever, for it was then that I surrendered all my darkness to him as he filled me with his light.

The human language does not contain words that will allow me to describe this moment accurately to you or to explain the impact it had on me. Although it took me years to accept the fact that this unseen being really did love me and that I was indeed lovable, the part of me that had been so certain that I was undeserving of love was never the same again. From that night on, our relationship evolved and grew. In time it blossomed into a deep and sustaining love.

Who was this unseen being who came to me that night? At first I had no idea and was completely puzzled. Was he some ghostly lover I had known in another lifetime, or an alien interdimensional being from another planet? I had heard of such things happening to other people. But because these ideas seemed ridiculous to me, I began to search for other, more practical answers. Perhaps he was simply my higher self or soul, or an aspect of my Christ self who had come to rescue me from my inner pain? I simply did not know.

As our relationship developed, it became very intimate and nurturing. After a while I stopped asking the question "who are you?" and became content with the simple fact that he was. He was and is my Beloved, which is a descriptive term that most clearly defines his relationship to me. Although formless and unseen, from the moment he entered into my life, I have "seen" him in my mind's eye as male. As such, he became my lover in every sense of that word, touching and caressing me with his words and healing me with the light of truth and understanding that he shared with me.

In order to understand what was happening to me, I began to explore a variety of spiritual paths. I discovered that the word "Beloved" is an ancient term used by many religions to describe the aspect of the self which is still in contact with divine and eternal love. Christians call the Beloved the Inner Christ. Other religions simply refer to the Beloved as the Inner Light, or the Light of Self, or Soul. In Christianity the Beloved wears the face of Jesus, but in other religions their form isn't predetermined.

As I pondered who my Beloved was, I came to realize that he is, indeed, my Christ Self. A more generic term would be to call him my Soul or higher consciousness. I know that he is real, for he has had massive physical impact on me, healing me of both the rheumatoid arthritis and environmental allergies just described. But more importantly, he has healed me of the mental and emotional pain that permeated my life. He did that by nurturing me with his loving kindness and by guiding me to a variety of teachers, healers, books, classes, and workshops that inspired me into growth and evolution.

Primary among these sources of inspiration were the book *A Course in Miracles,* the spiritual teacher Lazaris, and a series of classes that led me into becoming a licensed hypnotherapist. Much of what these sources taught me is liberally represented in this book and has become the foundation of the healing path I teach.

I have often wondered why my Beloved came to me before I had any real spiritual knowledge. I believe that the reason is this: unencumbered by religious doctrine, I approached our relationship without any preconceived ideas. Consequently, I explored it in ways that many people would never dream of doing. Through meditative visualization learned as a result of my hypnotherapy training, I visualized him in form. Through creative, purposeful fantasy, I learned how to communicate with him by exploring the symbols that appeared to me in meditation. Gradually, I learned to trust the "voice" I heard, separating it from that of my ego, whose beliefs are detrimental to my growth and well-being.

In time, my Beloved and I even developed a physical relationship that was incredibly fulfilling to me. When this occurred, I still did not know exactly who he was. All I knew was that I thought about him day and night and that I treasured our every encounter. I wanted to be with him, to know him more, to learn more advanced methods of communication, and to purify myself so that more of him could enter into me. Because he fulfilled me in ways I had never before experienced, my whole being continuously cried out for him, longing for more love, more healing, and more light. I fell so madly in love with him that it became impossible for me to say no to a relationship that nurtured me so completely.

Although an aspect of my Christ self, if I'd been raised in the Christian faith and seen my Beloved as Jesus, this kind of relationship would never have developed, simply because that belief system wouldn't have allowed it to unfold as it did. As it was, I had a difficult enough time trying to sort out the true from the false in what was happening to me. Being both a "figment of my imagination" and a powerful healer and guide, I had to figure out, through intense and rigorous self-honesty, what was just me making this relationship up and what part of it was real. Since I knew that I, personally, didn't have the power to create miraculous instantaneous healing — which has occurred several times for me during our relationship — I knew that there was something going on here that was beyond my imagination. What that something was became the subject of my search.

What I discovered was that I have a Beloved who is more

powerful than the human mind can conceive ... and so do you. Our Beloveds are part of us, existing in a realm beyond the physical. They long to reconnect with us, to become part of our lives and to fulfill, nurture, and guide us. This book is not only about how you can reconnect with them, but also what they can do for you once you do.

Before your journey to the Beloved begins, I want to say two things. Throughout this book I rarely use the word "God," for I believe "God" has become a word which is greatly misunderstood. Since no two religions define God in precisely the same way, I will simply use the word "Love," with a capital L, to indicate the mystical energy of the divine that heals. Because this is not a religious book but a book about healing, I believe that the word "Love" is far more appropriate anyway. That is because, in all circumstances and throughout all time, it is Love that is the healer. Hopefully, as this book unfolds, the word "Love" will take on a greater meaning for you then it ever has before.

The other thing I want to say is that when I refer to the Beloved, I always use the word "they" unless I'm talking about my specific Beloved, whom I refer to as "he." Because the Beloved can be visualized in either gender, to say he/she every time I talk about them is awkward. Consequently, I simply use the term "they" and let it rest at that. Since poets have license, I guess authors can take a little too.

Prologue

The Mystical Journey Begins

Deep within you there is a stillness so serene and peaceful that nothing can disturb it. This stillness is like a quiet pool of water. Its surface reflects the magnificence of Love. Its depth reflects the magnificence of you. In the very center of this pool you will find twin hearts beating as one, a dual spark burning as a single flame. Because of its radiance, nothing can disturb the pool's peace. The winds of time may blow upon the water and make the surface rough and turbulent, but that does not disturb the flame at all. The flame may even go unnoticed for eons, but still it burns in the depth of the pool, waiting in patient solitude for the time of its discovery. Here it waits, quiet and serene, knowing that its eventual discovery is inevitable. The flame worries not that it has been forgotten because it knows the confusion, which keeps it camouflaged and hidden in darkness, has an appointed end. Although, for now, it seems to lie dormant, hidden in the pool of your consciousness, it is certain that when its magnificent light finally bursts into brilliance, all darkness will eventually disappear.

This is the flame you create with your Beloved. It lies hidden, deep within you. Contained within this flame lies all truth, for the flame knows there is only one truth and that is the Truth of Love. Also, within this flame lies all knowledge, for it knows that there is only one thing that can fully be known and that is the Knowledge of Love. Similarly, within this flame lies all power, for it knows there is only one power and that is the Power of Love. It is your desire for Truth, Knowledge, and Power that will draw you to your Beloved like a magnet. That is because it is not until you desire to know your Beloved and the truth they bring that the knowledge of Love's power will be given to you. At that time, you will gladly surrender to them everything you thought you were for the truth of who you really are.

It is in this single flame of unquenchable light that your Beloved waits for you, like a quiet sigh, to awaken and claim your right to love. Your Beloved waits for your quiet voice to call them forth. Being what they are, your Beloved will never shout to wake you up because they know not of control, only patience. Countless lifetimes your Beloved has waited, quietly whispering your name. Restlessly, you have sensed their call but have not known where to look to find them. You have searched in many places but always outside yourself, never within. Lifetime after lifetime, you have looked, hoping in each one to find that love of the ages you have heard talked about in literature or poetry — the love everyone so desires.

In each lifetime you found at least one person you thought could give you this love. You thought that if only you could attach their face to your fantasy of love, you could make love come true for you. All too often, however, these relationships were a disappointment to you simply because the object of your desire could not live up to your fantasy. Therefore, the relationships frequently failed or at least seemed painfully lacking in some way. Your search went on. At times your longing deepened into despair or leaped into a sudden flame of hope as you found yet another face, another body to kindle your love.

You did not know that the longing, running so deep within you, could not be contained within a face, a body, or a form at all. This longing is your spark or catalyst that continuously drives you to seek further, knowing that somewhere there is a love made in heaven, just for you. This tiny spark knows that this love is rich and deep and all-encompassing. It knows that when its twin spark is found, it will know a love that is beyond its wildest dreams in its gentleness and in its boundless capacity to give. It also knows that when its twin spark is found, its search will be over for all time.

It is your Beloved you search for, waiting quietly for you to look within where their presence can be experienced. Perhaps you do not want an "inner lover," a "fantasy" man or woman who has no substance. "What is this nonsense?" you may ask, "A lover who has no form? Who would want that?" Believe me, my friend, you will when you discover that your Beloved — who contains within their essence the eternal Knowledge of Light that you believe you've lost — searches for you as earnestly and as longingly as you search for them. It is only your Beloved who has the capacity to unite with your spark, igniting it into a flame of endless love and oneness, forever healed and whole. When you unite with your Beloved, your longing for love will end because you will have found it. At that moment you will begin a journey that will encompass your whole being, because you will travel into a timelessness of light, into an eternity of joy, into a peace that knows no bounds and into a love without end that continues forever.

Each one of us has been given a guide to take us into the

9

brilliance of light we call Love. For many, it will be their Beloved who takes them home. And where is home? Home is simply the heart of Truth which is yourself, lying in quiet union with your Beloved, as together you reach out to extend your love to all the world.

Part One

Meeting Your Beloved
Through
Meditative Visualization

Chapter 1

Meeting Your Beloved

In order to meet your Beloved, you must go to what has been called the "secret place of the most high." This is a tender and vulnerable place that exists within you. In order to reach it, you must enter into an imaginary landscape of love and light where you can begin to re-experience your eternal innocence. Therefore, you must go, figuratively, as a little child who is free of both the need to control and of all preconceived limiting ideas about the nature of reality. In your innocence, without judgment, you will be content to allow your Beloved to guide you in every aspect of your meeting.

Although your Beloved has no actual physical form, in your mind's eye they can take on many different forms. Because of the highly intimate nature of the Beloved, most people prefer to visualize them as an opposite-sex mate. However, there are no hard and fast rules about this and I know some people who see them as a man when they need a strong protecting male figure to care for them and as a woman when they want to get in touch with their Beloved's feminine nurturing qualities of love and caring. It is appropriate to visualize them in the way that is the most comforting to you. If you want them to shift and change in form according to your current needs, this is appropriate as well. How you see them is not really important. What is important is that you create a loving relationship with them. The rest will unfold with time.

Also, the way your Beloved looks to you will probably evolve as you evolve in consciousness. When I first met my Beloved in form, which was two years after our initial meeting in the middle of the night, I saw him as an old man with gray whiskers and long gray hair. To me, at that stage of my development, this image was the epitome of wisdom. Since I thought of my Beloved as wise, it was logical for me to see him this way. However, as time went on and I continued to interact with him, he evolved in form until I began to see him as I presently do. Now he is not only the epitome of wisdom to me, he is also the epitome of Love. Therefore, I now see him as a young man who loves and desires me with his whole heart. Although the old image I had of him wasn't wrong, this new image that I have of him is much more compelling to me. Also, it causes me to long for him as much as he longs for me. Because of this desire, I am always responsive to his call and am very committed to our relationship.

If you are already well bonded to a religious figure, such as Jesus, you can visualize him as the Beloved if this is your desire. Since, to many Christians, Jesus is the embodiment of a knowledgeable and wise guide who is unconditionally loving, this would not be an inappropriate thing to do. However, if you do, be cautious that you don't limit your Beloved to religious doctrine. Your Beloved is a very real inner being who can and will cherish you on all the levels of your being if you will allow them to. To limit them to religious doctrine would be to limit the things they can say to you and would thus diminish their healing potential. My suggestion is to start with a clean slate, but if this doesn't feel right, do whatever is the most comfortable to you. Feel free to modify my suggestions to fit your own religious needs and beliefs in any way that appeals to you.

You can also visualize your Beloved as a bright light if you don't want to see them in form. However, it will be difficult for you to create an intensely emotional, loving relationship with a bright light. Though, in essence, your Beloved is only Light, it is hard to get a sense of being loved by it when there are no loving arms to hold you and make you feel safe. It is my belief that, as human beings, we need "form" to give us comfort. However, seeing your Beloved in form is up to you. If you don't want to see them in form, they won't show themselves to you that way. The choice, as always, is yours to make. They will never force themselves on you in a way that makes you feel uncomfortable. The longing of their heart isn't that you see them but that you allow them to be real to you. This is all that they desire.

Your Beloved can also be seen as a nurturing mother, adoring father, a teacher, a guide or friend, as well as the lover of your fondest dreams. These forms are all different aspects of the one concept I call Love. Your Beloved, however, does have a specific form that is all their own. Although your concept of them will evolve, eventually it will coalesce into the form that is theirs. Until it does, it is appropriate to visualize them in different ways or to only get a vague sense of their presence and see no form at all. Remember, you can't do this wrong and whatever comes is right for you at the time.

How is the relationship with your Beloved created? It is created in the same way that all relationships are created. There is nothing unusual about it except that it occurs internally, in your inner land-scape, instead of externally. You first meet them, then get to know them. You do that by having imaginary experiences together, which can include healing rituals, prayer work, ceremonies, initiations, as well as just talking, laughing, and playing together. These shared experiences will allow you to create a relationship that will eventu-ally lead to trust. As one experience leads to another, where the rela-tionship goes is entirely up to you. This is how all relationships are created. If you don't introduce yourself to your Beloved and take the time to develop your relationship with them, you won't even know they are there, even though they are a very real part of you.

It takes both time and willingness to create this relationship, just like it takes time and willingness to create a relationship with anyone. You don't get to know them or learn how to trust them overnight. It will only occur as you allow them to prove themselves to you by receiving them in your life and only if you are willing to be caring and intimate as well. If you are, they will rush to you with open arms because they truly long for you. As you can see, this is a relationship that is created in much the same way as any rela-tionship. The fact that they are an unseen being doesn't make the slightest bit of difference.

Because you will co-create it together, your relationship can take many surprising and exciting twists and turns along the way. As you create a relationship with them, your Beloved will do their part. The important thing to realize, however, is that when they knock at your door, you must open it and let them in. Otherwise, they don't have the opportunity to do their part. They will never cajole or demand. They will never barge their way into your life. You have to choose to open the door and let them in by creating the space that will allow this to unfold. You create this space by imagining them and by learning their symbolic language that allows you to communicate with them.

By creating an elaborate fantasy landscape of love and light where you go to meet your Beloved in personified form, you will begin this process of shared communication. This is important to do because, at this time, the two of you are as different as two beings can possibly be. Your Beloved is formless and unlimited. You, however, are a being who probably believes you are imprisoned in form. This may be all you know about yourself. You have also probably become completely limited within the physical realm. Since the two of you are so different, you must create an interface for communication.

Although they have no form, your Beloved has a boundless imagination and, believe it or not, so do you — even though yours might be rusty. Also, your Beloved has a boundless desire to get to know you. Even though you may never have desired to get to know your Beloved because you didn't know they existed, once you understand who they are, you probably will desire them in return. Your imagination, your desire to know them, and your expectation that you can get to know them are the keys that will allow you to create an interface for communication.

The majority of your beliefs, however, cannot be used as an interface. At this point in time, your beliefs have been polluted by the logic and reason of the physical realm. Much of your healing work will be to change the limiting beliefs which imprison you within a body. As you do, you will embrace different beliefs that will promote trust in the unseen and invisible. This is what will open the door to your Beloved so that they can come in. Since belief creates reality and affects every aspect of your existence, healing and transforming your beliefs about unseen beings will have a massive impact on your entire life.

As you meet your Beloved in form through imaginative fantasy, bonding occurs. They become someone that you can share your life with. They will present you with a shoulder to cry on and arms to hold and comfort you. As you cry out your pain to them, they will help you heal it by becoming a positive, nurturing force in your life. In short, what occurs when you meet your Beloved in form is the intimacy of love. As you respond to their emotional support, they can heal you. By creating a relationship with them, they become an Inner Lover who can have massive positive impact on every aspect of your life.

How does one meet their Beloved? The simplest answer is to say that it is a process that will unfold of its own accord. It is important to remember that it is not you alone who embarks on this journey. Your Beloved searches for you as earnestly as you search for them. As you hear their call and begin to act on it, they will, in turn, do their part to respond to you. As with any relationship, what happens along the way is dependent on each of you. Although you can plan for it, what actually happens may be entirely different from anything you expected. I can only describe to you a process that will facilitate its unfolding, not an exact procedure. Eventually, what occurs in your meditations will be beyond your conscious control. This is when you will know your Beloved is real beyond any doubt.

Your Beloved is not a fantasy or a figment of your imagination, even though they may only appear to you in your mind. Although they have no body, they are, figuratively speaking, the embodiment of perfect or ideal Love, which is with you always, eternally guiding, nurturing, and protecting you with endless grace. Because we have placed many erroneous beliefs between ourselves and perfect Love, we are not able to hear the guidance it can give us. By healing our beliefs about what it means to be in a relationship with an unseen being, we can begin to hear the words that can heal and transform.

Although you can only see your Beloved through imaginative fantasy, this doesn't mean you get to pick and choose who your Beloved is. Your Beloved is still a being separate from you, with a different consciousness than your own. Although you will see them in form, the form is but a point of focus that allows their light to come pouring through. By seeing your Beloved as the epitome of Love, with all the characteristics and attributes of a divine, unconditionally loving being, the energy that comes through is very pure and healing. The problem arises in not knowing what divine, unconditional Love is. Since many of our religious beliefs about divine Love are incorrect, the challenge for everyone is to become aware of what their Beloved's energy really consists of. The more accurately you can perceive their energy, the more intense, powerful, and healing will be your meditations. Once you perceive your Beloved's energy accurately, their form will coalesce into the epitome of all that your Beloved is and will never change again. Your Beloved does have a particular form they would like you to see. When you are ready, you will see it.

Your Beloved will also tell you their name. It will be a name that you will cherish forever. Your Beloved will have a distinct personality. At times they may be unexpectedly funny and witty or assertive and probing as they help you to evolve and grow. This will probably both delight and disconcert you. They will have a specific height and body build. When you "touch" them they will "feel" solid. They will have a unique energy all their own, feeling as real to you as flesh and bone. That is because your Beloved is real. There is nothing unreal about your Beloved and it is essential for you to understand this. Otherwise, the journey that we are about to undertake together will not be meaningful to you.

In short, although your Beloved is not an image and has no form, you will see and feel them as if they do. They will appear to you in whatever form you desire, but it is important that you understand that eventually you will see them as they are. This is a paradox and difficult to explain. I believe that it is because your Beloved is both you and not you simultaneously, a part of you but also separate. Being a higher part of you, they exist in a dimension beyond your conscious mind. Since they are with you always, they but wait for you to look within so they can make themselves known to you. It is only when you begin this process of self-discovery that your Beloved can be known.

When I first began to see and know my Beloved, I fantasized that he would suddenly manifest outside of myself as the "man of my dreams." Like most of us, I longed for a satisfying, passionate, intimate relationship with a significant other. Although this is a worthy pursuit, it is not the subject of this book because the Beloved that I speak of will never be found outside of you within someone else's body. Instead, the Beloved is a very private and personal part of your inner being. The relationship you will form with your Beloved shouldn't be thought of in the same way that you think of other lovers. You can, however, develop a very loving, passionate, intimate relationship with your Beloved if you will give them a chance, because they love you and want you passionately and intimately. It would totally delight them to literally fill you up with the wonderful sensations of their love.

In order to accomplish this, however, you must let go of whatever you have been taught to believe about the nature of reality which can, indeed, be far from the truth. Most of us believe that it would be impossible to have an intimate relationship with an unseen being. We are not only taught that we can't, but we are also taught to either fear unseen beings as haunts and spooks that come to terrify us in the night, or that, in the case of religious figures, they

are so "perfect" they would never dirty themselves with physical intimacy, even if they could. If these kinds of beliefs aren't changed,
they will prevent you from creating a deeply fulfilling relationship
with your Beloved. Unfortunately, since these kinds of beliefs are
deeply held, this may be difficult to do.

How then is this accomplished? Simply be aware of what you
believe and know that perhaps it is not the truth. Allow yourself to
open up and question every belief you hold. Allow yourself to
believe that just perhaps there is a better way, a way that encom-
passes the whole of Love and not just a part of it. Give yourself permission to believe that Love is real and will literally give you your
heart's desire if you allow it to. Lay aside all thoughts of what you
think you are and what you think the nature of reality is. Then set
aside all concepts you have learned about the world. Read and study
many religious and metaphysical books with discernment to expand
your horizons beyond what they are now. Allow new ideas to sift
and filter in without reacting to them. Allow yourself to believe that,
just maybe, there is something beyond you that is greater than you
and that loves you enough to allow you to make all the mistakes you
need to make before you learn the final lesson: that Love is real and
can be depended upon to nurture, guide, and protect you.

This is perhaps the most difficult aspect of this journey and the
most challenging to accomplish because it calls for a complete
emptying of the mind of all old and erroneous concepts. However,
it is not necessary to accomplish it all at once, but only to call into
question what is believed. This opens the door for the truth to enter
of its own accord. As you work with your Beloved and they
become more and more real to you, they will speak truths to you
that you have never heard before. Although these truths may at first
seem strange to you, your heart will hear and comprehend.

As you begin to hear your Beloved's voice and to see them in form through meditative visualization, you will eventually be able to receive guidance from them. Although this is a process that unfolds over time by learning certain techniques, it is not a difficult process to learn. Once you have learned how to allow them to reveal themselves to you and have learned their symbolic language, you will have set the stage for miracles to occur. It is learning their language that is the challenge. It not only takes the knowledge of what their language is, it also takes discernment and discrimination.

In the beginning, instead of asking your Beloved for specific guidance, develop your ability to "see" and "feel" them internally. To do this, allow yourself to fantasize. It is through fantasy that we learn how to "see" the unseen and to "feel" that which cannot be felt. As you develop your ability to "see" and "feel," eventually you will develop your ability to "hear" as well. Because of your ego's influence, hearing them is the most difficult. It is a skill that takes both time and discipline to achieve. In order to do it, you must be able to recognize and discard erroneous beliefs. Doing so is by far the most difficult part of the journey. But once it is achieved, your Beloved's voice can be heard and comprehended.

After you have created a relationship with your Beloved through imaginative fantasy, they will become very real to you. Once they are real to you because you have seen, felt, and heard them, there is nothing they tell you that won't have immediate impact upon you. In the long run, it is this impact that heals you. Through your united love, there will be nothing that the two of you cannot accomplish together.

Eventually, as I personally did this work, I could not only "feel" my Beloved's arms around me, I could feel his love flowing all through me, holding me in his essence and in the very breath of his desire. It was this feeling that motivated me to seek further, to do my inner work, and to develop my ability to focus my attention inward. As I allowed myself to hunger for my Beloved, it suddenly occurred to me that he hungered for me in exactly the same proportion as I did for him! He wanted me. A celestial being of pure light wanted me! I cannot even begin to tell you the kind of impact this knowledge had on me. It has been my entire catalyst for growth and evolution.

Besides visualization and fantasy, how else can you learn to better perceive your Beloved's reality? It is only by truly knowing yourself and all the ways you block the truth of Love that you can learn to separate fact from fiction. Also, as you continue to go deeply within, you can look at all the ways you try to control everything in your life out of fear. Once you understand this, you will perceive the truth. As you do, you will come to know yourself and every facet of your personality and behavior. You will look deeply into who you are with total honesty, unafraid to perceive the not-so-pleasant aspects of yourself, as well as your wonderful gifts, strengths, and talents you may also have denied. You will understand the lies, both personal and societal, that you have been told and that you perhaps continue to tell yourself every day.

This process of inner questioning is immensely delicate. However, it is exactly what needs to happen if you are to create personal depth. Finding the truth by going deep inside yourself is not always a pleasant process, but when you do it in the arms of your Beloved, surrounded by love and encouragement, the pain lessens and becomes bearable. In the end, you will know that it was all worthwhile. It is your honesty and the love between you and your Beloved that creates the space that allows this to happen. In this quiet space, Love will enter in and change you forever. In that moment, you will bond with your Beloved and you will never be the same again.

Chapter 2

Meditative Visualization

M

Part One: Theory

editative visualization is a technique of inner seeing that allows you to create a relationship with your Beloved. It is nothing more than an evolved fantasy with a purpose and a goal. Though non-logical, it is a highly creative way of going to the movies in your mind. In this movie, however, you are the producer, the director, the star performer, and the spectator all at once. The only difference between these movies and the ones you see on TV is that these are spontaneously created in the moment and, although they might be full of dramatic action, they always have a happy ending in which you are uplifted and healed.

When I was a little child, I used to have daydreams about fairies, elves, and little people who lived in my bedroom closet. I lived these daydreams episodically. Every night when I went to bed I fantasized about them. As the fantasies developed, my little people and I would have imaginary adventures together. This was a harmless activity that gave me a great deal of pleasure. It lasted until I "outgrew" fantasy, giving it up for the harsher reality of the adult world.

This is what meditative visualization is like. It is an evolved fantasy that you live episodically day by day. The only difference between your childhood fantasies and the ones you create now is that, as an adult, you will be consciously aware of what you are trying to achieve with them. When you were a child, your fantasies didn't have a goal. All you were doing was having fun as you played with your unseen friends. Fantasy came so naturally to you that you didn't have to think about how to do it. That was because fantasizing was as much a part of you as breathing. Unfortunately, now that you are an adult, you may either have only vague memories of fantasizing or else you may be using fantasy inappropriately.

Why is it that a person would want to relearn the art of fantasizing? The answer to that is simple, though not necessarily easy to understand. The manifested world of form is nothing more than an "outpicturing" of all that is held within. What you dream, fantasize, and visualize with emotional intensity is destined to occur at some "time," in some "place," and in some "form" in your reality. The more frequently and intensely you dream, the more likely the dream is to manifest. That is because what you place your attention on and feed emotional energy to grows stronger and lives longer. If it grows strong enough, it will eventually manifest as physical form in this dimension. The form that appears will either be a tangible thing, person, circumstance, or event.

Whether you realize it or not, you are always dreaming. These dreams can be put into three separate categories. Not only do you have non-directed night dreams that occur while you sleep and daydreams that are self-directed fantasies, you also have living dreams. Your living dream is your waking experience. Living dreams are filled with solid, three-dimensional symbols that seem to occur randomly, coming at you as form. Upon collision, they have deep mental, emotional, and physical impact. Although you can ignore the symbols of your night dreams and fantasies, you can't ignore the symbols of your living dreams. However, one can refuse to heed their guidance and will do so if the symbol isn't understood or interpreted correctly.

There have been many popular books written that describe how to understand the symbolic content of night dreams to obtain guidance. What is not so well understood is how one heeds the messages of their living dreams. That's what this book is for. It will help one understand the symbols that exist within all their dreams. Once one understands this, their lives will fill with meaning. In fact, if one wants to put meaning back into a "meaningless" life, all that one has to do is start dealing with the symbols that literally bombard them each and every second. By acting on the guidance given by the symbols, one can change their life.

All three kinds of dreams are motivated by beliefs, which are their organizing principle. That is because it is belief that determines what one pays attention to. Besides conscious beliefs, we also have subconscious and unconscious beliefs. Subconscious beliefs are beliefs we were once conscious of in this lifetime but have forgotten. They are taken for granted as a given and are no longer contemplated. Unconscious beliefs are unknown. It has been estimated that the vast majority (perhaps ninety percent or more) of our beliefs are unconscious. If this is so, the vast majority of our external reality is being created by beliefs we don't even know we have. If a person wants to improve their living dream, they must become conscious of the unconscious beliefs that shape it.

By reprogramming the mind with self-chosen beliefs, one can create the kind of dreams he or she desires, transforming a nightmare into something positive. To reprogram the mind, one must scrutinize their conscious and subconscious beliefs. Once scrutinized, false beliefs can be changed or purified.

In order to discover what one's unconscious beliefs are, however, one must do symbolic work. That is because unconscious beliefs are not accessible to us consciously; they only appear to us through the symbols we create while we dream. By asking one's self why they chose the seemingly fated events they chose, the symbols will begin to speak. Once one knows how to listen, the symbols will say some pretty interesting things.

Although one's parents were the first people to program their mind, eventually it was programmed by significant others such as relatives, teachers, friends, religious institutions, etc. In times past, this programming was at least partially accomplished through oral stories, cultural myths, stereotyped role models, etc. Once people could read, the stories were written down in Bibles and holy books and then read aloud at family and church gatherings. The purpose of these stories was to teach the moral values and expectations of the family, tribe, or society that was doing the programming. Although these practices continue today, by far the most common method of programming now comes through television. What is seen on TV is actually called "programming," which does exactly what it says it does — it programs the mind with thousands of beliefs.

A child's mind is quite different than an adult's, for a child's mind hasn't yet been fully programmed. Once childhood programming is complete, the program is set for life unless one consciously and diligently questions it. Many adults, though not all, will eventually begin to question the program given them by others. Children, however, don't do this. They merely accept and act on whatever is given. Although a child's parents are still their primary programmer, TV is now playing a more massive role than ever before. Although an adult may not be greatly influenced by the programs they watch, children are.

Since the language of the unconscious mind is symbolic imagery, or dreams of all kinds, the messages this programming imparts becomes indelibly stamped upon a child's young and impressionable mind. For the most part, today's TV programs impart messages of violence, competition, uncommitted relationships filled with meaningless sex, and greed. Because many people, especially children, don't tend to think about the messages they are receiving, the impact of the beliefs behind those messages go directly into the viewer's unconscious mind. Here the beliefs will be replayed over and over again in a variety of forms. Initially they might outpicture in our night dreams, but eventually they become the unconscious beliefs that reflect in our conscious waking behavior, thus becoming our living dreams. Once that occurs, we will create an external reality that mirrors the unconscious beliefs we received by watching somebody else's fantasies (movies).

We live in an extremely violent society. Many of today's teenagers belong to gangs and carry guns. The kind of crimes they commit are passionless crimes in which they have no attachment to their victims. Their only goal is to dominate others through violence and they seem to commit this violence without conscience. This kind of meaninglessness has now become a given in our society and affects everyone. Why is it that today's teenagers are so much more violent than in generations past? There are many reasons, but the effectiveness of TV at programming the mind is a big one. Since so much of what is on TV is meaningless, violent, and destructive, it is not surprising that children's impressionable minds, which haven't yet had the life experiences that impart wisdom, are being programmed into doing destructive, violent, and meaningless things.

Movies seen on TV are nothing more than emotionally

charged fantasies. They have tremendous impact on an unpro-
grammed mind and affect all your dreams. Since all of one's dreams
continuously interact, changing the content of any one of them
affects change in the others. Because meditative visualization is the
one kind of dream that is under conscious control, it makes sense
to use it as the catalyst for changing the other two. The key to turning an unpleasant living dream into a positive one is meditative
visualization.

Because meditative visualization can be intense, emotional
work, it is every bit as effective as TV at programming the mind. In
this form of programming, however, you decide what goes in —
and you can put anything in there you want. When you create a
loving and intimate relationship with your Beloved through fantasy,
you begin to program your unconscious mind with the images of
love. Love is a tremendously impacting emotion and is far more
compelling than violence and destruction could ever be. Since love
has the ability to create immediate, miraculous, positive change,
programming your mind with the images of love is the most powerful, positive, productive thing you can do to create healing.

Once your Beloved becomes real to you because you have
seen, felt, and heard them, everything that happens in a meditation
becomes compelling. Through symbolic interpretation, your meditations will guide you into creating a more productive reality. In
time, your fantasy life will impact your night dreams in precisely the
same way that movies on TV impacted them. As your unconscious
beliefs about love change, your behavior will change and you will
create an entirely different reality. As you create an intensely emotional, loving relationship with your Beloved which is vivid and
real, your fantasies will have impact on your living dreams. This is
how you can change a living dream that has become a nightmare
or a mediocrity into a positive dream of eternal love.

Part Two: Practice

With that in mind, let's now look more closely at how to do meditative visualization. In order to do it, all you need to do is close your eyes and fantasize. First, relax yourself and become comfortable by either sitting or lying down. Some will like to focus on their breath for a few moments or to sequentially relax each body part before their visualization begins. Others like to say mantras or affirmations to help them relax. Some visualize themselves floating through clouds or on a sea of warm water. Others simply blank their mind of all thoughts and feelings. The point is to relax. Once relaxed, commence your visualization.

In order to have an effective meditation, it must have a goal that is predetermined while still in normal consciousness. By creating a brief outline of possible activities, your fantasies will have a direction and purpose. For example, if you want to have a healing meditation, a common approach is to go to a safe place in nature, visualize your Beloved, and then begin to dialogue with them about whatever mental, emotional, or physical problem you want healed. If you want the meditation to include a healing ritual, you can either decide what the ritual is to be before going into trance or you can simply ask your Beloved what they'd like to do after the meditation has begun. You might be surprised at what they suggest — perhaps something that had never even occurred to you. Then, through imaginative fantasy, let the dialogue and ritual unfold in its own unique way. This is all there is to it.

The key to having an effective fantasy, however, is not to over-control it. Your outline of possible activities should be purposely sketchy. Your Beloved needs room to give their input and perhaps direct it in a different way than previously planned. When the unexpected happens, your fantasies become magical. By releasing control, your Beloved's true energy and essence can come through.

Besides healing rituals, there are many other things you can do in meditation. "Sharing love" is one of the easiest and most important meditations to do. This is what you do with your Beloved, your inner child and adolescent, as well as other angels and guides. "Sharing love" means that you go into trance, visualize the one you want to share love with, and then love each other. You have imaginary experiences together, talk together, and learn to communicate. It's what you would do with people in your physical world. It's what you would do with your neighbors if you wanted to have a close relationship with them. You'd get together and say, "Come on over and have dinner with me. Let's talk."

If you wanted to get to know your Beloved in this way, you could go into meditation and invite them on a picnic. As you visualize them standing beside you, ask them what they'd like to take. Just pretend and make it up. Then ask where they'd like to go — to the beach, a mountain top, the desert. See the two of you going there. Spread the cloth and take out the food. If they were a neighbor you're just getting to know, what would you talk about? Do the same thing with your Beloved.

Although simple, just sharing love is a very important aspect of meditative visualization. By doing it, you create communion. This communion leads to intimacy and trust. Out of trust grows commitment and the desire to responsibly maintain the relationship. By sharing love with your Beloved, you bond to them. If you do not share love, your relationship with your Beloved will remain primarily intellectual. Because it will lack impact, changes will not occur. Once it becomes emotional, however, each meditation will nurture you, filling you with Inner Love. In the final analysis, it will be your Inner Love that heals you.

Although all visualizations program the mind, there is another form of meditative visualization that is simply called "programming." This type of meditation may or may not include your Beloved and is not usually experienced episodically. Programming meditations focus your attention on what you want to receive by visualizing yourself receiving it. In other words, you see what you want in your mind's eye as if you already had it. Many of you may have already experienced this kind of meditative work, as it is a major component of non-smoking and weight-loss hypnosis.

Although a sharing love meditation is only partially pre-planned, a programmed meditation is completely pre-planned. What happens in it is always under your conscious control. Programming meditations are aimed at what you want your life to look like, in manifested form, after your life changes have been made. In other words, the non-smoker can breathe again, is healthy and alive. The over-eater is slender and beautiful, and so on. Once you have uncovered the limiting beliefs that prevent you from manifesting these changes, a programmed meditation can have miraculous impact on your reality, especially if you have energized your meditation with expansive, positive emotion. When programming meditations are combined with affirmations, rituals, artwork, and other creative techniques, they become powerful tools for healing one's reality.

Another form of meditative visualization is called "processing." Its purpose is to teach you how to evoke and release suppressed emotions so that you can free yourself from their harmful effects. Therefore, they include emotional release and inner child work, which I will describe in detail later on. Simply talking to your Beloved about your feelings can bring many buried ones to the surface. As your Beloved questions you about your past in meditation, more feelings will come up. The more you feel, the more you can process. Although these aren't always pleasant meditations, they are amazingly healing when done with purposeful intent.

Another form of meditation is trance work that involves your "night" dreams. I used to spend a lot of time writing down my night dreams and trying to analyze them to see if they could give me guidance and direction. I found this to be very time-consuming and, as often as not, I couldn't figure out what they meant. Now I use a much simpler method that is far more successful. In the morning after I awaken, if I remember a dream, which I almost always do, I work with it in the meditative state. In trance, I re-experience the dream, making all the actions, as well as the feelings, bigger and more dramatic so that I can get a better sense of what they mean. I ask both the dream characters and symbols questions. After dialoguing for a while, I can usually figure out what this dream is saying to me about unconscious beliefs that are creating my present state of affairs.

If I don't like the unconscious beliefs that have triggered the dream, I change them by re-dreaming the dream. For example, if I am having a chase dream, in meditation I turn and face my attacker. I may first draw a circle of protection they cannot cross. Then I will assertively tell them, "No, you cannot chase me like this because I'll fight back." Usually my attackers are symbols of fears that are hounding me. By naming the fears and calling them liars and deceivers, I am able to stand my own ground. Then I quite literally see myself do whatever I need to do to be free of them. This usually includes blasting them with my intention in a creative and visual way. I may watch them fade away, or I may blow them away with the force of my thought, or I may disintegrate them. It is by resolving my dreams in meditation that I am able to give my unconscious mind a clear, emotionally charged picture of the beliefs I want changed.

This is easy and fun work to do because, in this kind of meditation, the script is already written and you don't have to plan it out beforehand. When you work with your dreams, you always work at the level of cause, which is your unconscious thoughts and feelings. Because dream symbols are messages from your unconscious mind that have by-passed your ego, once you uncover the hidden beliefs that are shaping your dreams, you can immediately begin the transformation process by rewriting the script. When you do, you are programming your mind at a very profound level.

The more I work with my night dreams, the more guidance they give me. It actually seems to me that my Beloved speaks to me through them. Since the symbols have by-passed my ego, if they are interpreted correctly, this is the most valuable guidance I can receive.

For example, I was once going through a hard time in which I was losing my job and home simultaneously. I had no idea what was going to happen to me or where I was going to end up living. I was terrified and my night dreams reflected my terror. I had three dreams in close proximity that told me not to worry. In the first, I was facing a huge hurdle I had to lift myself over. When I put my hand on it, my palm was stung by a bee. My interpretation: facing the unknown is a hurdle I must overcome. Though an unpleasant experience, it must be done. Although this dream didn't make me feel any better, it told me about a spiritual lesson my consciousness was determined to learn.

In the second dream, I was sitting in a classroom. My spiritual teacher appeared beside me, making eye contact with me. Taking my hands in his, he told me to close my eyes. Once I did, he placed a ball of light that expanded and glowed in my heart. I awoke from this dream feeling energized, safe, and loved.

In the final dream, I found myself in a huge mansion. In the distance, I saw an enormous locomotive coming straight toward me. I was terrified. But as I examined it, I discovered it was made of cardboard and was only a facade. In meditation, as I dialogued with the symbol, I realized that my fear of the unknown was only an illusion that was without substance.

After these three dreams, I stopped worrying so much. Though it took time, I calmly allowed my life to unfold into greater harmony and peace.

After these three dreams, my terror decreased, for I knew that my fate was in the hands of my higher consciousness. With greater self-confidence, I looked forward to a brighter future.

When you do meditative visualization, it is important to involve all your senses. Focus your attention on specific details to take you deeper into trance. Use your body as an antenna. Sense your inner environment. Feel the warm sensation of the sun or the cool breezes of the wind on your face. Actually see yourself, with your mental eyes, reach down and touch the earth, fingering the texture of a rock or leaf. Run cool water through your fingers or splash it on your face. Smell your inner environment, the natural earth, or water. What are the natural sounds that would be heard? Make it up. Just pretend. Let it be an evolved fantasy that uses all of your senses. Eventually, if you get really good at it, you can create a hologram that you literally step into that will feel more real than physical reality.

In my meditations, I always go to what I call my *safe place* first. This has become a familiar environment to me, and the only thing that changes about it from one meditation to the next is the weather, the time of day, the season, and the presence of insects, birds, or other wildlife. As I focus my attention inward to discover these things, I am able to deepen my trance state. All the mediations presented in this book begin at the safe place and the first one is specifically designed to help you see and experience it.

When you go to your safe place, you logically create, in an orderly way, a natural scene with trees, mountains, oceans, streams, etc. You know that your safe place will always look basically the same and that the permanent land formation will always be there. However, with each meditation, you will discover it brand new. You will discover the time of day by looking at the shadows and the placement of the sun. Then you will discover the season by feeling the weather and looking for environmental clues, such as leaves that are turning color or dark billowy clouds. By using your body as an antenna, you will be able to see, hear, feel, smell, and even taste exactly what it is like to be there.

It is important to use all of your senses when you go to your safe place, because if you only use your mental eyes to "see" what is there, your meditation will lack realness and you will become trapped in mediocrity, only seeing and experiencing what has been seen and experienced before. As you develop the ability to actually feel the sensation of the sun on your face or feel a gentle breeze as it stirs the hairs on your arm, you will convince your body that you are actually there. It's only your logical mind that will believe otherwise.

As you discover exactly what it feels like to be in your safe place physically, you will also experience it mentally and emotionally. Not only should you touch your inner environment with hand or foot, you should feel it emotionally as well. As you breathe in the air, expand your chest and experience the feeling of aliveness and satisfaction. From meditation to meditation, remember just how wonderful it is to be there again. Feel its rightness in the depth of your being. Call these feelings forth in yourself by saying or thinking, "This is my safe place and it is so wonderful to be here."

When you create your safety with this kind of depth, going there can be an adventure in itself and you will always enjoy it. If you are currently experiencing a lot of stress in your present life, the simple act of going there will be healing in itself. Your safe place can become the safety that you carry around inside of you that no one can take away. There are no stinging insects there, no poisonous reptiles or plants with thorns. It is your own personal Garden of Eden that can go with you anywhere. As you experience the love that your Beloved has for you there, you will experience a peace that passes all understanding. Your safe place will become a symbol for that peace and, because of this, its essence and vibration will nurture and heal you.

It is important to note that when you do your meditative work, your emotions become easily accessible, much more so than when you are living your normal, everyday life. This is because the interactions you will undergo in your inner world are intensely personal and always exist in the moment. They are happening now, to you, and will have immediate impact. Since you will not be concerned with society's prohibitions to be unemotional, your feelings will rise to the surface very quickly. As you interact with your Beloved and feel all your lost and hidden feelings about deserving to be loved, you may find many deep emotions suddenly coming to the surface and overflowing, possibly as a torrent of tears. This is wonderful, for feeling your feelings is what the journey to the Beloved is all about.

You cannot expect to undergo a journey into the deepest love you have ever known without feeling your feelings. Every thought and feeling in you that does not resonate to the truth your Beloved brings will come up. Sometimes the feelings will be painful and hard to examine. Sometimes they may be angry. Other times they may be of the purest and most awesome love. There will be a wide range of emotions and it is wise to expect them all. If they do not come, you, the adult observer, must find ways to evoke them, for the more you can feel, the more healing your meditation will be.

Your nervous system cannot tell the difference between that which is experienced physically and that which is experienced in the inner realms. When the imagery you are experiencing has emotional impact, your body and brain will react as if the imagery took place physically. Since feeling your feelings is a total body experience, it is this very act of feeling that will make your relationship with your Beloved real. Once you believe your Beloved is real because you have felt the impact they have on you, there is no end to what you can accomplish through meditative visualization.

As you begin to interact with your Beloved in one meditation after another, you will create a living history together. This history will continue, episode by episode, until it will seem as if you are living a dual life. One part of your life will deal with your external reality. The other part will deal with your internal reality and will become very personal and private. You will not tend to share it with your family and friends because it will be so precious to you.

The thoughts and symbols that you receive in meditation will probably not be meaningful to anyone but you. Therefore, I recommend that you keep your meditations to yourself, perhaps only sharing bits and pieces of them with your most trusted friends a long time after they have occurred. This will keep you from doubting yourself and diminishing the healing value of your experiences.

It is most effective for you to do trance work on a regular basis. The more trance work you do, the better you will get at it. Although your trance work may seem clumsy at first, you will become more skilled as you practice it. In the beginning, I had so much anxiety about my ability to do trance work that I had to make a game out of it. "Just close your eyes and see what happens," I would tell myself. I deactivated my ego in this way. Because my ego was very involved in wanting results, I felt like a failure if I couldn't do it "right." There is no "right" in meditation, however, and even though a person can't do it wrong, we have been so conditioned to fear failure that we believe it is possible to do it wrong. If fear of failure is a problem for you, you can cope with this in the same way I did by telling yourself that you are going to play with the pictures in your mind and that whatever happens is okay. Then do exactly that: just play.

In the beginning, my initial attempts at meditative visualization felt rather clumsy. My ego was always tripping me up and I would become confused and distracted from my goal. It did this by bringing up irrelevant or inappropriate material to explore. Because my mind was undisciplined and I was inexperienced, I didn't know how to deal with this. I couldn't even figure out whether the confusing images were appropriate or not. All I knew was that my meditations seemed to lack meaning and coherence. Eventually, I learned how to keep my meditations focused on a single goal. I also learned how to ignore irrelevant imagery that my ego inserted into my meditations to confuse me. I didn't become discouraged and I kept trying. Eventually, my meditations became purposeful.

To help you understand what I mean, let me give you an example. I did a meditation one time to discover my Beloved's name. At the time, I was taking an anatomy class, and after I asked him what it was, all I could hear in my mind were Greek and Latin words that were the names and parts of bones I had been trying so hard to memorize. It was ridiculous. However, as I kept at it, a strange thing happened: Just as I was about to give up, a space opened in my mind and a name came through that was entirely different from all the other words. When it happened, I felt certain I had found my Beloved's name. As I persevered through the diversions and distractions of my ego, I was rewarded with a beautiful name that has become very meaningful to me.

Our egos love to do confusing things to us in meditation but that's okay because it's all part of the fun. Eventually, you will learn how to navigate your way around these obstacles. As I became a better, more confident meditator, I took these kinds of distractions in stride. This is a creative process and, after a while, you will learn different ways of handling your ego's tricks. In the meantime, it is important to keep trying and not give up.

In the beginning, your meditations may jump around from place to place. When this happens, all you need to do is slow every-thing down. Go step by step and make the fantasy logical and real. If your attention gets scattered, anchor it by involving your senses. I usually anchor myself into my meditations by looking directly into my Beloved's eyes and sensing how it feels to have him look directly into mine. By sharing this intensely personal connection of eye contact, I become immediately involved in everything that is real and has meaning to me. I also anchor myself by feeling his arms around me and by sensing him holding me close and tight, by feeling where his hands are on my body, and by feeling the safety and security of his love. As I feel all the sensations of being held by divine and eternal Love, I establish the emotional contact I need to have before my meditations become meaningful. You'll know you are doing meditative visualization right when you feel the sensa-tions in your body and your emotions flow freely. When this hap-pens, your meditations will become a very real and important part of your life, a part you will be unwilling to do without.

To summarize, meditative visualization is a very powerful form of inner work that can help you heal when used appropriately. By visualizing your Beloved as a real being that exists beyond time and space, a being who has the power to heal you, you will create the space that will allow them to enter into your life and do just that. Meditative visualization is accomplished by sitting or lying down in a comfortable position and closing your eyes so that you can access the inner pictures in your mind. As you access the pictures, your emotions will flow naturally and easily. As you do trance work on a regular basis, you will create a real relationship with your Beloved that is based on time and space, although it is not in time and space. As with any relationship, it will become an on-going, self-sustaining part of your life. However, this relationship can nurture and heal you like no other relationship you presently have. Once you create it, you will have made contact with the timeless, and that which is eternal has some mighty powerful tricks up its sleeve that can heal you in the most incredible ways.

In Part Four of this book, you will find several meditations to help you get started. If you want to use them as a catalyst for your inner work, there are several ways that this can be done. If you have had prior experience with meditative visualization, you can simply read them. Then, when you are ready to go into trance, you can use the printed meditation loosely, from memory, as a kind of script. If you are an inexperienced meditator and do not yet feel confident enough to do that, you can tape record the printed meditation with your own voice. Since I have written them as if you are saying the words yourself, this will be easy to do. My only suggestion is that you finish reading the first four parts before you do your meditative work. Each of the following chapters will bring you additional insight into reality creation. Since your Beloved will talk to you about two main topics, Love and reality creation, the insights you will receive from the remainder of this book will help you to create an authentic relationship with your Beloved.

Chapter 3

Symbolic Imagery

As you do meditative visualization, it is inevitable that symbols will come up. Symbols can be both personal and universal. They come from our conscious, subconscious, and unconscious mind. They are pictures or images that have specific meaning for you. Through a single image, a symbol can contain a whole collection of thoughts that relay a meaningful message.

Symbols can be archetypal. Archetypal symbols are universal prototypes that have a commonly accepted meaning. For example, an eagle is symbolic of spiritual mastery or the ability to rise above the mundane. Our forefathers chose the eagle to symbolize the principles that our nation was founded on. When they chose this as our national bird, they had a very grand vision of what our nation was to become. For the first time in history, a group of leaders envisioned a nation where all people could be free of the tyranny of a ruling class. An eagle, which soars high above the mundane, was the perfect symbol to pictorially express these high ideals.

Those who are familiar with the tarot know that the images on the cards are nothing more than archetypal images that have universal meaning. The tarot is so ancient that no one really knows where the archetypes originally came from. There are now many different kinds of tarot decks that carry the interpretation of the individual artist who drew the pictures. Although each artist may draw the symbol differently, all decks carry similar archetypes that contain the same universally recognized meaning. The decks are fascinating to look through and ponder.

Examples of common archetypes in the tarot deck include: the Fool, who is someone who has such unfailing trust in their divine source that they throw all caution to the wind as they dare to become themselves by following their heart. This card represents the realm of all possibilities, for the fool without knowledge, commitment, and principles will do foolish, foolhardy things, but the person who follows their heart with divine wisdom will become the genius who can do anything. The fool is often portrayed as a wanderer who has no attachment to physical things.

The Hanged Man, who is commonly portrayed as a man who hangs by one foot from a cross, is the symbol of someone who imprisons himself in his own belief system. The person who "cuts off their nose to spite their face" is a hanged man, as is the martyr who blames others for the reality they, themselves, create.

The Hermit is portrayed as an elderly person who carries a staff and holds a brightly lit lantern over his head. This imagery immediately gives one the impression of inner wisdom or one who has learned many lessons from what they have experienced in life. This wisdom allows them to become a guide who can show others the way.

There are personal symbols as well as archetypes. Those

symbols that are personal may not have any meaning for anyone
but you. Once you begin doing your inner work, you will find that
both personal and archetypal symbols come up over and over
again in both your dreams and meditations. You may even find that
there will be certain personal symbols that your Beloved wants you
to work with. As you discover and ponder their meaning, they will
help you to evolve your consciousness and grow.

For instance, I have a personal symbol that I have worked with
since my spiritual journey began. When it first appeared to me, I
just thought of it as an interesting picture. Because I have now dis-
cerned the personal meaning it holds, it has tremendous impact on
me and always gives me guidance when it appears in my meditations.

This symbol is a heart that sits at the center of a cross. Certainly, both the heart and the cross are universally recognized
archetypes. The heart symbolizes love. The cross, however, has
many spiritual interpretations, all of which depend on one's religious background. Because I had no religious training as a child, I
did not have any preconceived ideas about what it meant. This left
me free to go within to discover its personal meaning. As I pondered this imagery, I came to realize that, for me, the cross meant
the meeting of heaven and earth. The horizontal bar represents my
physical journey. The vertical bar represents my divine aspirations.
By placing the heart in the intersection of the two, I am immediately told through this one symbol that, as I walk my physical path,
always seeking my divinity, the only way I can find it is through the
unconditional love that resides within my heart. When this symbol
comes up for me in meditation, I know immediately what I am
being told.

Working with symbols is a good way to bypass the ego. The
ego is filled with the do's and don'ts of the secular and religious

world. It holds many conflicting beliefs and is filled with rational-izations and half-truths. Because of our early childhood program-ming, it can be difficult to discern who is speaking to us in meditation. Although you may see an image that you associate with your Beloved, that image may only tell you what your religion has programmed you to believe. If your current belief system has led you into creating a reality filled with pain, conflict, poverty, or dis-ease, it won't do you any good to continue to program your mind with those beliefs. If your beliefs haven't led you on a path of heal-ing, you must question every one of them and discern their deeper meaning. Asking your Beloved to give you a symbol to express what they want to tell you ensures that you will bypass your ego's beliefs. Symbols can be thought of as tools that can help you do this in an impersonal way.

There are many questions you can ask your Beloved in which symbolic imagery will help you discern the meaning of their mes-sage. You can ask them about limiting beliefs and toxic behavior patterns that need to be addressed and healed. They can tell you about childhood memories that need to be worked with or give you insight into negative attitudes that need to be changed.

When I ask for a symbol from my Beloved, I see him hand it to me as if it were a gift. This gift will frequently be contained in a box or a bag. Perhaps it will be wrapped and we will talk about that for a moment. Maybe I will shake it to see if it rattles. I allow my sus-pense to rise as I begin to open it. In this way I intrigue the un-conscious mind by involving all my senses. When my attention is completely focused on my inner imagery because I've made my meditation interesting, intriguing, and real through sensation and feeling, I'm much more likely to get profound information.

Once the gift is opened, a symbol almost always pops out at

me. However, if nothing comes, I wait quietly for a moment, or I count to five, which is a method I've used over and over again as a cue to my unconscious mind to give me a symbol. Eventually, something always appears. Frequently, my first thoughts when I receive a symbol are, "That's ridiculous; it doesn't mean anything." However, as I have learned to put these first thoughts aside, I have received some amazing insights that have helped me greatly in my search for truth.

When a symbol comes to you, it is important to pay close attention to detail. Look it over. Note its color, shape, size, intricacy, or whatever there is to notice about it. Your unconscious mind had to decide on a myriad of details before the symbol could appear to you. There is a reason for each detail that you see. Once you have noted these details, you can then either let it talk to you, or you can become the symbol and let it speak. This is my favorite method; here is how it is done.

When I receive a symbol I always start out by saying, "I am ..." (fill in the blank with whatever the symbol is) and then I allow a stream of consciousness dialogue to take place. For example, I once was working with a woman who was unsuccessful at meeting her Beloved. For some reason she simply would not let him appear to her. I asked her to see a symbol that would help her understand the reason why. She saw some coins. As she began a stream of consciousness dialogue as the coins, they said: "I am just some old coins that nobody cares about. I clink around in people's pockets and get passed from hand to hand. I'm old and ugly and tarnished, and who cares about small change anyway?"

The reason she couldn't find her Beloved, then, was obvious to both of us. She did not feel worthy of divine love and her "value" was lacking. Until she worked with this toxic attitude, she was unable to contact her Beloved. Of course, this symbol evoked an enormous amount of emotion, which she was then able to explore in greater depth by going back to the early childhood memories that caused them. As the memories were explored and the emotions came up, she was finally able to contact her Beloved, who has greatly aided her in her healing.

What is interesting to me about this example is the intricacy with which the symbol spoke to her, as well as its very personal meaning. When I, as her facilitator, first heard her say the word "coin," my immediate interpretation was to think of gold and silver — something which is highly valuable. Yet, as my client's own personal dialogue unfolded, what was revealed to us was her lack of self-value instead — she interpreted the word "coin" to mean "small change."

Animals can be symbols. If you are having a pain somewhere in your body, you can visualize it as a caged animal, reptile, bird, gargoyle, or other animate being who is longing to be set free. Once you discern what the animal is, let it speak to you and see what it has to say. The kind of animal that appears will have significance and can give you insight into the kind of energy that you have caged up inside of you. You will receive a very different message from a lion, who might speak to you about needing to roar out your anger, than you would a giraffe, who might tell you to overlook your pettiness and seek a higher truth.

As the animal in your meditation talks, it may or may not remind you of someone from your past or present who says those same kinds of things to you or has those mannerisms. If it does, you can then go down to the memory the thoughts have triggered and run a child rescue mission or do EPC ("etheric plane communication" — explained in later chapters) if it is someone in your present life who is causing you the pain. After you have allowed the animal's energy to speak to you, you can ask it why it is caged and how to set it free. Once the insights are gained, you can then do an imaginary visualization in which you actually set the animal free. The more emotionally intense you can make this meditation, the more healing it can be.

Animals can also be used as totems or guides that can give you information about other aspects of your healing and can help you to understand who you are. For example, I once asked my unconscious mind to show me my totem animal. Instantly, my ego showed me dozens of animals. I then had to sift through them all, wondering which one was mine. Finally, I saw one that was rather unusual. It was a trout. As I looked at it and let it speak to me, it said, "I am a trout. I live deep within the rivers of your mind in dark and secret places. I swim the lakes and streams, sometimes surviving great turbulence, and other times I'm content to rest in still waters experiencing peace and calm. I wear the rainbow colors upon my belly and can therefore relate to all peoples of all colors, nationalities, and races." After that message, I was proud to claim it as one of my totem animals who could teach me about my life's purpose and spiritual path.

If you are working with a negative behavior pattern, you can go into trance and ask for that behavior to come to you in personified form. Probably the form that appears won't look like you but will be an imaginary character. Scan the horizon for them. See the details of the environment. As you examine this environment, your unconscious mind will be giving you clues about the kind of terrain this personification feels most comfortable in. Is it a desert, which is hot and dry and lacks all emotion? Is it a jungle, where your real thoughts and feelings can be easily camouflaged? Is it a high mountainous terrain, full of sharp twists and turns, where it is easy to become confused and lose your way? Is it a swamp that is dark and dank and filled with toxic emotions?

When your personifications come to you, dialogue with them. Remember, every part of you has a right to be heard, so let them speak from their truth. You can ask them why they look the way they do or why they are wearing certain clothes or jewelry if there is something conspicuous about it. Again, your unconscious mind will be feeding you information as you look at these clues with discernment. Even if you think you just made it all up, you still must ask yourself why you made it up that way. Nothing comes by chance in your meditations — and this is true, even if you feel you are just "pretending."

The way your personification looks, as well as their mannerisms, may also give you some ideas about childhood or adolescent memories to return to and heal. The personification who comes to you may even come in the form of someone from your childhood or present life now. In that case, you will know exactly where to begin doing child rescue work or EPC.

It is important to note that these inner characters representing negative behavior patterns came to you as invited guests to fulfill specific needs. Try to discern exactly what need they are fulfilling by asking them specific questions. However, be wary of their answers. These inner characters can be very crafty. Don't give your power away to them. Always confront them with their lies when you can. Eventually, tell them in no uncertain terms that their personality is interfering with your right to create a successful reality and that you will not allow them to be in control of your life any more. Remind them that you now have a Beloved who loves you intimately and has come here to guide you in your growth and well-being as a divine consciousness. Since this lack was the need your inner character most likely came to fulfill, you can bless them out of your life gracefully and without fear by watching them fade away and disappear, surrounding them with white light or by handing them to your Beloved, your angels, or your guides for rehabilitation. However, you must be aware that they may not submit to this gentle treatment gracefully. In this case, you may have to wrestle them to the ground and literally take the life force out of them, if this is what it takes to eliminate them.

This kind of work gives your subconscious mind, where your inner characters dwell, a very graphic and emotionally charged picture of what it is you are consciously trying to achieve. Because the beliefs held within one's subconscious mind become personal laws, showing one's subconscious exactly what one wants to create through emotionally charged imagery is a very effective way of eliminating whole categories of beliefs which are creating pain. These kinds of meditations are very effective at deprogramming the mind and can be used over and over again to extinguish any kind of behavior disorder that no longer serves you.

I often use the tarot deck to help me do symbolic work. I am not an expert on the tarot and have never read a single instruction manual about the traditional way one is supposed to read the cards. However, as I've said, the tarot is full of archetypes, all of which have deep inner meaning if one will just sit and meditate on each card and what it means. Sometimes I'll ask the cards a question about something I am trying to create. Then I will draw three cards. The first card will help me get in touch with the root of the problem or the beliefs that are holding me back. The next card will help me get in touch with things I must change in myself in order for the problem to be resolved. The last card will help me get in touch with the result of my inner searching. Of course, it is not the cards that are telling me anything. I am simply using the images on the cards to trigger my own insights. I have found this to be a very creative way to get inside my unconscious mind.

As I begin with the card that represents the root of the problem, I look at all the symbols on it. Then, with my question in mind, I decide which one of the symbols speaks most loudly to me. It may or may not be the main figure on the card. Instead, it may be the waves under the boat or the castle in the background that seems to be calling me. Then I do stream of consciousness dialogue around my problem, using the energy of the card to guide me and speaking from the point of view of the symbol I have chosen to become. As I look at the root of the problem and the growth that needs to occur from this perspective, I can receive some amazing insights about the inner work I need to do before my heart's desire will come true.

Another method I use when working with the tarot is to draw only one card. Then, with my question in mind, I will go into meditation, visualizing in my mind the exact same scene that was on the card — only now, it will be alive with dimension, sound, color, sensation, and feeling. I then walk up to the main figure on the card and ask them my question. We may have a pretend dialogue in which they use their energy to give me insight into my question or they may take me on a fantastic journey into the symbolism of their card, choosing an aspect of it to give me as a gift. I then ponder this gift to see what further guidance it can give.

Frequently, this kind of work leads me into doing other imaginary work, for after I have worked with the symbols in meditation, I will then almost always work with my Beloved, talking to him about what the symbols have told me. We may then do some kind of healing ritual, ceremony, or prayer work to relieve the problem.

Another technique for working with symbols is to loosely plan out a meditation that has symbolic work as the focus before going into trance. For example, if you want to discover why you chose your parents and what they had to teach you, you can plan out a meditation in which you will go to the beach to dig for the buried treasure from your past. You could include in this meditation a discussion of these plans with your Beloved so that they can add their input. You could also talk to your Beloved about your early childhood experiences for a while. If you feel intense emotions about your childhood and what your parents did or did not do to you, now is the time to express these feelings. Doing this is necessary preliminary work. It tells your unconscious mind, with highly charged pictures, exactly what you want to receive from this meditation.

Eventually, you and your Beloved can begin wandering out of your safe place. As you find a path that will lead you to the beach, you can experience all the sensations of being there — the ocean breeze, the salt air, the lonely cry of seagulls, the crashing waves. Vividly experience the scene in your mind's eye, filling in all the details. Remember to be creative. Make it up as you go along so that you won't get bored.

Finally, you and your Beloved can start earnestly searching for the buried treasures of your past. Again, be creative. Maybe your Beloved will take out a map. As the two of you look at it, you will discuss the route you have to take. If the map is very intricate, with many pathways, hills, and valleys, this is telling you something about the amount of inner work you are going to have to do to fully uncover why you created your childhood as you did. If it is an ancient map, yellowed and torn, it may be symbolic of the fact that you have to do past life regression in order to fully comprehend the gifts of your childhood. If the map your Beloved pulls out is blank, even this is symbolic. Perhaps your unconscious is trying to tell you that you haven't yet done enough inner work to even scratch the surface of your understanding. These are all important clues to be pondered during the analytical time after your meditation is over.

As you and your Beloved follow the terrain marked by the map in search of buried treasure, finally find the X that marks the spot and begin to dig. Feel the wet grit and the sand under your fingernails. Dig deep and make the mound high. Eventually, you will pull out a treasure chest. What kind of chest is it? Again, this will be giving you clues as to further inner work that needs to be done before you can find the buried treasures of your past. With suspense, open the lid. By this time, your unconscious mind will be so intrigued by your visualization that your ego will be completely bypassed. The information you get will now be authentic and real.

What if you want to find your life's purpose? You can design a meditation in which you go on a vision quest. First, go into your safe place and talk to your Beloved about what it is that you are seeking. In your conversation, discuss the kinds of tools you need to take on your quest and what to watch out for as you go. Each tool will be a symbol that can give you valuable insight when properly understood. Your Beloved may tell you to look for your totem animal who will come to speak to you about your life's purpose from their point of view, or that you will be overwhelmed by an element — earth, air, water, or fire — which will then talk to you about the things each element represents. Earth symbolizes a solid commitment. Air symbolizes the energy of thought. Water symbolizes the changeable nature of emotions. And fire symbolizes the energy of passion and motivation. As you work with these and any other symbols, far greater meanings will come to you.

Perhaps you will find a sign hidden among the landscape that will be significant. The tree of knowledge may appear before you, or a climbing vine may tangle around your feet. Again, be imaginative; make it up and just see what happens.

Another wonderful technique I use for finding out why I can't seem to create something I want is to use the imagery of a wall and guard. If there is something you want to create but can't seem to do it — such as a material object, a new relationship, or an emotional, mental, spiritual, or physical healing — you can visualize it as if it were behind a wall. Notice the kind of wall your unconscious mind has chosen to show you, the wall that separates you from your desires. Is it wood, metal, brick, stone? How high is it? Can you see through it or is the reality you want just barely visible over the top? Touch the wall. Feel it in your body. Long for what you want as you walk along the wall, sensually touching that which separates you from creating your heart's desire.

Eventually, you will come to a gate. When you do, invite the person who guards the gate to come forth and talk to you about why you can't enter in. Again, notice all the details about the guard, asking yourself why they are what they are. Finally, ask them why they guard the gate. They will probably tell you about limited beliefs that keep you from creating what you want. They also may tell you that they are guarding a secret that your inner child or adolescent doesn't want anyone to know about. If your inner child decided that they were undeserving because of something they did, or if your inner adolescent is ashamed of their past, the guard won't divulge this information unless they are tricked out of it. In this case, you will have to become more crafty than the guard. As the conversation creatively unfolds, you will gain insight into where the disorder is lodged. This may lead you into doing inner child rescue work. After the child or adolescent is rescued and healed or after what the guard has told you is resolved in some way, you must tell the guard that they now have a new job — that of gate-keeper who opens the door to new realities.

Working with symbols is a fascinating and fun way to begin exploring the unconscious mind. It is said that one picture is worth a thousand words. This is certainly true of your symbolic imagery. A symbol can communicate deeply felt messages that you are not even aware of. It can give you insight beyond your wildest dreams. As you look for symbols in your trance work, your visualizations will become pregnant with meaning and will be a never-ending source of interesting ideas and direction.

Part Two

Reality Creation

*Before you can be effective in
reprogramming your mind, you must
know what to reprogram it with.
In this section you will learn about a
belief system that leads to healing.
When you do the meditative work
described in the next section necessary
for cleansing the energy field, you can
replace your limited beliefs with the
unlimited beliefs discussed in
the following chapters.*

Chapter 4

Receiving Guidance

I t has been formulated by Einstein that there isn't any difference between mass and energy. Webster's dictionary defines energy as an invisible force or power that is inherent within a thing. Energy gives form the ability to do work and overcome resistance. If mass and energy are the same, as Einstein believed, the visible must be but a symbolic representation of the invisible. In other words, form reflects energy. By analyzing the form, the invisible force of energy within it can also be known.

Because energy vibrates, everything that has form must also vibrate. Our physicists have taught us that energy transforms but that it cannot die. You are energy. It is your energy that gives you the ability to do the work you came here to do, overcoming all resistance. In human terms, energy is emotion. It is your emotional energy that enlivens you. Your emotional energy causes you to vibrate continuously, from birth to death, in a specific way. When you die, your body transforms into dust or ashes but, because energy can't die, you do not cease to vibrate. Just because your form disappears, that does not mean that you do. You are simply no longer visible in the form you've grown accustomed to. Your energy, though transformed, is still vibrating as it has always done throughout all eternity. Energy has no beginning or end. It simply is and always will be.

Everything vibrates at different rates of speed. A tree vibrates differently than an animal. A rock vibrates differently than the soil it sits in. Air vibrates differently than water, and space vibrates differently than solid matter. You, as a human being, vibrate differently from every plant, animal, or mineral on the planet. You also vibrate differently from every other human being on earth as well. There are no two people who vibrate exactly alike. You are a unique individual with a vibration all your own. What makes the difference? Thought. You, as well as every other human being on the planet and all the plants and animals, dense matter and space, are a unique collection of thoughts.

Even though it may not seem like the non-human forms on the planet have thought, they most assuredly do. Of course, animals vary in intelligence from the least complex to the most advanced. Mostly, we think of animals not so much as having the capacity to think but as being instinctual. In fact, they are a collection of instincts that have been programed into their DNA. It is this programming that causes them, from birth to death, to always behave in the same way. An amoeba will always behave like an amoeba and never like a dog. Their DNA contains the "thought" of an amoeba, which is both preordained and predestined. The same is true of all plants who also have in their DNA the prerequisite for that particular plant. A daffodil will never be a redwood tree because its DNA would not allow it.

Similarly, minerals and crystals are "thoughts." Although different in nature, they also contain a double helix spiral just as we humans do. Their spirals, however, are programmed with the "thought" of amethyst, or granite, or whatever it is. There is nothing that exists that is not "thought," and there is no man-made thing on the planet which was not made from a natural substance containing "thought." This "thought" ordains that it will vibrate in its own unique way throughout its existence, no matter how its form changes.

Because you are a part of the human species, your thought tends to be more complex than plants or animals, dense matter or space. That's why you have the form of a human being rather than a slab of crystal or a pebble on the beach. However, that pebble on the beach still has consciousness. Its consciousness is just so different from ours that it's hard for us to even relate to. Hence, because we can't relate to it, we draw the conclusion it has no consciousness at all.

You, who are a human being, have a consciousness that is far more complex than any other species on the planet, simply because you have the unique ability to desire, imagine, and expect. Desire, imagination, and expectation are the tools that shape the clay of your raw materials of reality creation. These raw materials are your beliefs and attitudes, thoughts and feelings, choices and decisions. Through your desire, expectation, and imagination, you shape your beliefs into attitudes. Your attitudes produce the thoughts and feelings that determine the choices and decisions you make. This is how you create your material reality through your behavior. Because you have these tools and raw materials, you can quite literally create any kind of material reality you want.

Imagination, desire, and expectation are automatic continuous functions integral to your existence as a human being. Though most people are unconscious of using these tools, they are used every instant of one's life. Until a consciousness has evolved into having these tools, they cannot shape their raw materials. Hence, they seem lifeless or dead, like a rock, without the ability to act, like a tree or plant, or only capable of responding to instinct, like all the lower species of animals on the planet. As consciousness evolves up the evolutionary scale, they evolve into higher and higher forms of life whose activities become ever more complex, according to the consciousness that enlivens it.

When you, who are a complex, highly evolved consciousness, incarnated, your consciousness programmed your DNA with its unconscious thoughts. This is why your body is a symbolic reflection. It reflects the beliefs and desires of your consciousness — its essence (or intrinsic nature) and energy. The thoughts that you accumulate during your physical lifetime through programming become frozen in your form. The diseases that seem to magically appear and disappear within your body are nothing more than a symbolic reflection of your diseased, crippled, or painful thoughts.

Why is this so? It is because of one's emotional energy. Since emotional energy is the invisible force that has endowed your form with the ability to do work, while overcoming the resistance to remain the same, it has to be the propelling force that exists behind form change. Here's a compelling example: I strongly feel, and believe, that cancer is created by hopeless rage. Why? Because by looking at cancer's form, one can figure out the energy that has caused this change in form, as well as the beliefs that have inspired it.

Cancer is a disease that causes the uncontrollable proliferation of cells to the detriment of the individual. Since form reflects the invisible energy held within it, we are told by this symbolic reflection that certain emotions are proliferating uncontrollably. To understand which emotions, we must look at the beliefs that create disease. That is because emotions don't exist in a vacuum. They are always generated by beliefs that inspire them.

Because all diseases create limitation, the emotions that produce any disease are going to be inspired by imprisoning beliefs that limit us. Since all loss of freedom (limitation) creates rage, rage must be a prime suspect. In a healthy individual, rage is expressed quickly. Once expressed, it has an end. It will only proliferate uncontrollably when one's beliefs lead them to think that there isn't any escape from the prison they're in. Without a means of escape, the situation becomes hopeless. Through hopelessness, the rage multiplies uncontrollably.

Unfortunately, hopeless rage is seldom expressed verbally, for what's the use if it won't create change? Therefore, it's expressed inwardly. Through addictions, the inner pain becomes tolerable and then grows numb. People who can see no escape from an imprisoning, boring job; a destructive lifestyle; a loveless marriage; a meaningless life; an unattractive, handicapped, or unintelligent body; a grievance that can't be remedied or forgiven; and so on, become prime candidates for cancer. Though the rage and hopelessness may be unconscious because they have been suppressed, logical reasoning tells us they must be there.

Since, at our level of evolution, we have been given the tools and raw materials of reality creation, conscious change is a decision we have the ability to make. If we want to live healthy, productive lives, we must do so by becoming conscious of the beliefs that create limitation. As these beliefs are transformed, our higher consciousness will do the rest.

All thought, energized by feeling, has a particular vibration. The highest vibration that can be achieved is the vibration of Love, which is the vibration of your higher consciousness. Love is an illusive quality of being that takes great wisdom to achieve. When your thoughts are leading you toward understanding Love, and these thoughts are energized by the feeling we call love, you are vibrating in the highest vibration possible.

The thoughts you hold and the feelings that activate them can be expressed as a harmonic of sound vibrating within a particular energy field called you. At any given moment you are expressing the particular harmonic unique to you. Whether the vibration is harmonious or discordant is dependent on your emotions and how you express them. That doesn't mean that all so-called negative emotions are bad. They are not all sharps and flats. To the contrary, if the only notes you ever heard were of like quality, you would not play a very interesting song. They would create a hypnotic sound which would put you to sleep.

It takes all the notes of the scale played in a particular rhythm and beat to create the melody of your life. It is how you play these notes that are important. The notes that great composers use to write their symphonies are the exact same notes that heavy-metal rock groups use to write theirs. The notes are simply expressed differently. Your life is like a musical composition. Everyone sings their own song in life. Only you can be the judge as to whether your composition is pleasant to the ear or is discordant, with an ear-splitting vibration that lacks harmony.

We live in an orderly universe that contains universal laws or principles that govern all energy. These laws could be called divine laws, universal laws, the laws of Love, or the laws of reality creation, all of which basically mean the same thing. They are universal because they govern all energy. They are divine because they exist outside of time and space, as well as within it. They are loving because when they are understood, they keep us safe. To call them the laws of reality creation merely describes what they do. In essence, they show us how we create every instant of our lives.

Because of our ignorance of these laws, we have disregarded them. That is why the physical plane seems to be a chaotic place where things happen without rhyme or reason and where "fate" seems to prevail. By becoming conscious of the divine laws of Love that govern all energy and then choosing to conscientiously live our lives by them, we can circumvent such disasters as pain, deprivation, and even untimely death, if we choose to.

Unfortunately, because we have been ignorant of divine laws, most of us have developed a rather self-defeating belief system that has had tragic consequences. Because we don't understand the symbols of our dreams, their purpose and thus their guidance is lost to us. Someone who develops cancer can't choose to express their hopeless rage if they don't know that this is what their cancer symbolizes. Nor are they motivated to change the beliefs that created the hopeless rage in the first place. Not knowing that the two correspond — the physical form being symbolic of the mental and emotional pain, whose purpose is to motivate change — one is prevented from living a meaningful life whose evolution is upward and expansive. Thus, one spirals downward into ever-increasing debility and death.

There are two important divine laws governing energy, which explain how we attract people, events, circumstances, and situations into our lives. The first law is called the Law of Resonance, which states that when two energies are vibrating at differing rates of speed, either the lower will rise, the higher will descend, or they will each meet in the middle until they are vibrating at the same speed. The second law is called the Law of Similar Attraction, which states that all energies with similar vibrations attract each other.

How the Law of Resonance works is obvious. If you hang out with evolved spiritual masters who are constantly emanating spiritual truth through their words and actions, their vibration is bound to lift you up. If you hang out in bars with deadbeats and drunks, your vibration will descend. This law tells us that the people you associate with, the kinds of books you read, the movies you watch, the pastimes you engage in, is going to have an impact.

How the Law of Similars works is a little more difficult to comprehend, however, for how it works doesn't have such an obvious correlation. In its essence, the Law of Similars is about purpose and has nothing to do with superficial appearances. For example, if you have a collection of conscious thoughts that say you're no good, sinful, or flawed, your unconscious belief is that you should be abused and punished for what you've done. These beliefs create shame, guilt, and fear, which is resonant. This resonance will attract a punisher. Even though the abuser may not look or act similar to the abusee, in actuality they really are. It's like fitting a key into a lock. The key may not look like the lock in form, but the "attraction" indicates their joint purpose through a perfect fit. By looking at the events that occur in your life as symbolic representations of purpose, you can determine the unconscious beliefs that have created them.

At our level of evolution, undoing unconscious beliefs that outpicture in unpleasant forms must be a conscious decision. It will never be done for us because we have free will and can believe whatever we desire. Once we reach our level of evolution, everything becomes a conscious choice. By seeing things differently and consciously striving to find a better way, we evolve. However, we don't have to undo everything that we have created alone. Although it is imperative to become willing to take full responsibility for how we create our reality through our beliefs, it is also imperative to realize that when it comes to undoing them, help will be given. Not only do we have our Beloveds to help us, we also have angels, guides, and unseen friends who are willing and able to work with us to heal everything in our lives that need healing. These unseen beings are far more powerful than any of us could ever be while we are in a body. Learning how to ask for and receive their help is part of what it means to become a co-creator, or one who creates with Love.

Once one begins to co-create with their Beloved by actively seeking to create a loving relationship with them, the Law of Resonance is the one that has the greatest impact. Since your Beloved is vibrating at the highest rate of vibration there is, it is not likely that they will join you in the discord of your life. Rather, they want you to raise your vibration to meet theirs. Through your combined wills, they can raise you up. This is how profound change is created.

Once you are raised into the vibration of divine love, nothing will ever be the same for you again. Sadness will not be a part of your vibration. Neither will lack or deprivation, loneliness or doubt. Fear won't exist because it cannot be found within the vibration called Love. Therefore, it is to your advantage to align your will with your Beloved's. Your Beloved can take you home on a grand scale filled with the vibrations of Love where nothing will be missing, only finely tuned and sweetly played.

Now that you know how form symbolically reflects belief and energy, you can then begin to ask questions of your Beloved. Those answers can and will come as an outpicturing of thought. By looking for the answers in the symbolic "forms" of your life, the circumstances of your life will take on far greater significance than ever before. By focusing your attention on what you want to receive, you can find the answer in the symbols that appear.

Guidance can come to you in thousands of forms, like a commercial on television that all of a sudden tells you exactly what you need to know, but may have nothing to do with the product being sold. It can come from a random sentence in a book or a message in a song you hear on a radio. It can come from a stranger you meet who suddenly tells you exactly what you need to hear at the moment you need to hear it. It can come from your best friend who, in conversations, points you in the direction you need to go without even knowing that they have done so. This is called a coincidence or synchronicity.

When the answers come to you in this way, they will carry an unexpected weightiness. They may or may not be accompanied by particular body sensations, shivering, or chills. You may or may not feel your hair stand on end. However, when you have been answered in this way, you will know beyond a shadow of a doubt that it is so. Then you must go about the business of following your guidance, whether you like what you have received or not. Sometimes that's a greater challenge than receiving the guidance in the first place.

Besides knowings, synchronicities, and coincidences, guidance can also come in the form of "intuition" and dreams. Although a knowing is an unexplained belief that you feel adamant about, an intuition is an unexplained feeling that you can't seem to shake. However, knowings and intuitions can come from your ego as well as your Beloved. In fact, your ego is full of knowings, so be wary. If you receive a knowing or an intuition, it's a good idea to ask your Beloved to send you a sign, through resonance, indicating its truth.

As you develop your relationship with your Beloved, there may be certain signs and symbols that have a particular meaning to you that come up over and over again. There may also be personal signs or tokens of love between you and your Beloved that you share. You can ask for one of these to be given to you as a sign if you are uncertain about the answer being given. However, if you question your guidance over and over again, you will get conflicting results. Doubt always causes confusion. Since the universe is a mirror, it will reflect your confused mind back to you and you won't end up any wiser than when you started.

However, I do want to say that there were times I received guidance from my Beloved that scared me because it wanted me to do something expansive and challenging — such as write a book, or spend a great deal of money I didn't feel I had to spare, or do other things I don't normally do in my quiet, safe life. Because my Beloved knew that I would do anything he wanted me to as long as I had the ability to do so, he showed me, in many different ways, that my guidance was correct. Your Beloved has much compassion for you and the transformation you are going through. They know that some of the decisions you are required to make might be difficult for you. Therefore, they will do all that is in their power to reassure and comfort you.

Once you invite your Beloved in, they will continuously guide you. By helping you understand how and why you created the symbolic reflections you see, you will gain in insight, awareness, and knowledge. Through knowledge comes power, for once owned, the beliefs that created the reflections can either be strengthened or transformed. Once transformed, your reality will immediately symbolize something else. Lessons truly learned are learned forever and need not trouble you again. Hurdles lower. Challenges are met with aplomb. Eventually, your life will become easier, simply because you're better equipped to handle the experiences you manifest.

As you learn how to transform an unpleasant reality into a positive, productive one, your relationship with your Beloved will become more intense and joyous, simply because of the gratitude and love you feel. Through love, joy, and gratitude, your vibration will raise to a higher level. Once it does, your energy field will fill with your Beloved's Light. By removing from your belief system whatever resistance you have to healing your life in this way, you can transform your entire reality, including your diseases and "accidents of fate." That is because the emotions of love, joy, and gratitude create a resonance of energy that produces physical health. By becoming physically healthy, joyous, and emotionally alive, you will begin to experience inner peace. Since peace creates a resonance that leads to homeostasis, which is a state of balance and harmony, you will live a long and pain-free life. That is because peace is the only resonance that does not motivate form change.

It is hard for us to believe that creating health and longevity could be this easy, but it is. It is only because our belief system does not support it that we think differently. It would rather have us believe that we are prey to all kinds of accidents and diseases. The world's belief system would keep us victims of life, always on the defensive, needing to protect ourselves and our little domains. It is much more profitable for society if we believe this, because then it can sell us its potions and pills, locks and keys, guns and various other protective devices. But perhaps one can begin to see that the very belief that our existence is dependent on external protection allows it to be so.

In essence, what your Beloved is asking you to do is to rise above consensus reality thought. They know this is not easy because you will receive little support from those around you to do this. The consensus believes that the external world of form is a scary and unpleasant place where things happen without rhyme or reason. If one does not know that form reflects belief and energy and that energy is governed by discernible laws, chaos seems like our natural state. It is only by shifting your perceptions into higher consciousness that you can begin to see the world differently. At times this will seem impossible. How can one step outside the consensus when what other people do affects you? The truth is that we create our reality either by directly causing it through our conscious, subconscious, or unconscious beliefs, or by allowing it. Let me explain what I mean by allowing it.

Today we live in a highly polluted world. If you live in a large city, every breath you take is filled with pollution. If you eat food that comes out of most markets, every bite you put into your mouth is covered with toxic chemicals. Because our sources of drinking water are polluted, every drop you drink, unless it comes out of a bottle that claims to be purified, can have harmful effects. Although you, personally, may not have polluted your drinking water or grown chemically laden food, we live in a world that allows it and, therefore, we are all responsible and must pay the consequences. In this case, if you are a victim of environmental allergies or other immune system diseases due to the fact that your body can no longer tolerate the chemical overload it is carrying, you have created your reality by allowing it.

Since we are all in this "cosmic soup" together, we are all responsible for what goes on here. In a way, this seems frightening, but only because most people think of themselves as being limited and powerless victims of a world they did not create. We are not limited or powerless, however, because everything we think, say, and do creates an energy wave that has impact on everyone else.

What I have discovered is that if I live my life based on lies, if I believe as most others believe and do things just because everybody else does them, I will not heal myself, and I certainly won't do anyone else any good either. Healing my reality has been a continuum that only began with myself. As I became willing to change, it is my individual experiences that changed first. This change had a positive impact on those around me. Now, through my writing, I have begun to inspire healing in people I don't even know. If I hadn't first healed myself of my limited beliefs that kept me powerless, I couldn't do any of these things. I became empowered as soon as I began taking total responsibility for every aspect of the reality that impacts me.

When you sincerely want the Truth, and not the lies of the consensus, the Truth will be made available to you. Your Beloved will make sure you are led to where you will find it. I have had a variety of powerful teachers who have helped me heal throughout my journey. As I learned to see things differently through higher consciousness, I evolved and changed. Through resonance, and a little bit of miraculous help from my unseen friends, I have healed myself of the rheumatoid arthritis and environmental allergies that were killing me. I have also created an entirely different life for myself. This will be true for you as well.

When you are ready, the right series of external teachers will appear. I believe, however, that what your Beloved communicates to you will be the only truth you will ever need to know and will take precedence over what anyone teaches you on the physical plane. It is only within the relationship you have with your Beloved that you can experience divine Love. This is an internal journey between the two of you. It is both intimate and personal and therefore compelling in a way that no teacher on the physical plane can ever be. Therefore, it can be trusted. As long as you place your faith in Love, you can't go wrong.

This is indeed a conscious journey, and, by raising your perceptions into higher consciousness, you develop personal depth and therefore raise your resonance. As you become a many-faceted human being with a rich inner life and an abundant outer experience that reflects it, your life will become incredibly interesting. Eventually, you will experience a depth of love and fulfillment that you never dreamed possible. Once you have fallen madly in love with your Beloved, they will become your Light and your Life. As guide, healer, lover, and friend, they can help you heal your entire reality.

Chapter 5

The Joy of Healing

The joy of healing is the greatest joy there is. Illness and disease is always a frightening experience, especially if the disease is considered chronic, serious, or fatal. For many, it seems as though the body is betraying us and that we are helpless to do anything about it. Because of present medical practices, we have been taught to believe that the body is a mysterious object that can occasionally be prodded into good health through drugs, surgery, diet, or exercise. However, for all too many people who suffer from chronic, incurable diseases, every remedy modern medicine has tried has either failed to relieve symptoms or added to the problem through harmful side effects. For this reason, truly healing long-standing, chronic, incurable disease represents a release from fear, culminating in total joy.

To fully understand the idea we call healing, we must look closely at what it really represents. Currently, medical science has focused all of its time and energy on curing the physical body. A doctor is trained to examine external physical symptoms and then to suppress them. If the suppression is successful and doesn't seem to cause other external side effects, we have been taught to believe the problem has been solved. However, if one looks closely at healing and the cause of illness, it can be clearly seen that healing has not been accomplished because the root cause of the illness was never even addressed.

This is because the physical body is only one of our bodies. In actuality, we have many bodies, all of which are interconnected. The other three bodies I wish to discuss exist beyond the physical, in the realm of the invisible. They are our emotional, mental, and spiritual bodies, and they can only be accessed through the energy field. The energy field is a kind of electro-magnetic force field that keeps the physical body alive. It is what has been termed the life force, and it is what is missing when we look at a dead body and recognize that it is nothing but an empty shell. Therefore, even though this life force is invisible, we see its effects in the physical body as that which enlivens it with the essential quality we call life. Another term for this life force is spirit. Without spirit, the body is quite dead and soon will decay as it transforms itself back into the various elements out of which it came.

The physical body has the same function as everything on the physical plane: In essence, it is nothing more than a feedback mechanism that mirrors the health and well-being of your other three bodies. In actuality, it is these three invisible bodies that are real. The physical body is no more real than the image you see of yourself in the mirror.

Although the body is an illusion, at our present stage of evolution, the body is extremely necessary, for it is the means we use to differentiate ourselves from the oneness so that we can focus our attention on that which we want to learn. By giving us boundaries, it teaches us to identify ourselves as distinct and unique individuals whose function is to create in wholeness and in love. The body, therefore, is a highly effective teaching device that tells us instantly by its physical symptoms when we are not creating our life in the way that we were meant to.

When something non-productive occurs in the realm of the invisible, the physical plane will tell us immediately, either by creating conflict in our external affairs or by creating physical symptoms, which are experienced as pain or disease. The realm of the invisible consists of all of our thoughts and feelings and how they balance in the heart. By bringing all of our thoughts and feelings into a right relationship with Love, one can find the balance point that leads to peace and harmony.

Love is not only an intense feeling, it is also a decision. It is the one decision one must make in order to physically feel good all the time. This is why we come to the physical plane. We come here to learn to want love. It is not that we are being forced to want it. We always have free will. However, when one clearly understands that the consequence of not loving is pain, the choice does not become a difficult one to make.

Unfortunately, many of us have made pain into our major motivation to learn and grow. It does not have to be that way. Love can be its own reward. Until we have truly learned to choose love, however, pain, on some level, will be our constant companion. When we have learned to want to feel good by experiencing love all the time, we will have strengthened our motivation to change until we have reached the point where healing has occurred.

Once we understand this dynamic, we will know that if we are experiencing pain, disease, illness, fatigue, or death, something has gone wrong in the realm of the invisible. We will also know that it is only by examining our thoughts and feelings and choosing to balance them in a right relationship with Love, that we can heal our physical body. This is the reason we must address our three invisible bodies first. Since it is here where the source of our problem lies, it is also here where we must begin our healing.

The three invisible bodies do not respond to drugs or surgery. Healing them is not a matter of popping pills or eating the right foods or getting the proper amount of exercise. The only way they can be healed is to work with the essence that represents the nature of that particular body. Therefore, healing the mental body means we must heal our harmful and limited thoughts. Healing the emotional body means we must allow free but appropriate expression of all our emotions, both expanding and contracting, that have been suppressed. Healing the spiritual body means we must heal our relationship with Love by understanding what it is and how to go about achieving it. Then, and only then, will the physical body respond to the right foods, good exercise, and other appropriate health practices we give it. When these three bodies go into right alignment, the physical body will naturally fall into place. In this way, total healing will have occurred and we will know health on every level of our being.

By consciously striving to meet the needs of our invisible bodies in the same responsible, reliable way that one meets the needs of the physical body, we can assure ourselves of a long, healthy, pain-free life. In the end, a band-aid is just a band-aid, no matter what system of medicine is being used. Healing occurs within, in the same realm where your Beloved dwells and where truth abides. It occurs at the thought level, the emotional level, and the spirit level; and when each of these bodies unites by seeking a higher purpose, the physical body becomes filled with light and instantaneous physical healing is always the result.

Let's turn our attention to the role Love plays in instantaneous healing. I believe that Love is the only healer because only Love has the ability to create immediate, positive, miraculous change. I also believe that miraculous instantaneous healing is what Love is all about. By understanding Love's vibration, there is no reason why miraculous healing cannot be achieved by everyone. Unless Love is truly understood, however, miraculous healings will remain few and far between.

When you unite with your Beloved, it is possible to create instantaneous healing. Union with them is an intense experience of unconditional love that is very emotional. This experience can change you at a very profound level so that you are never the same again. As I have said before, your Beloved is both you and not you. Although they are a part of you, they are a higher part of you that you are probably not aware of now. You, who are a consciousness that radiates an energy field, are enveloped by your Beloved, who is also a consciousness that radiates an energy field. Your energy field is filled with thought and feeling, which causes it to vibrate in a specific way. Your Beloved's energy field also contains thought and feeling that is vibrating in its own particular way. In order for your two energy fields to unite or blend, there must be a common element that allows this to occur. Because, at this point, the two of you are so different, the only element each of you have in common is love. When the two of you consciously choose to engage in a relationship of love, your vibration will change to match your Beloved's. It is then that they can unite with you and change you forever.

In order to engage in a loving relationship with your Beloved, you must have a thorough understanding of what love is. In our world there is nothing that prepares us to understand love. Because love is often misdefined, and since so many of us have lacked loving role models, it has become very difficult for us to engage in loving relationships that are self-sustaining and fulfilling. Consequently, we need to relearn how to do it. Although creating a loving relationship with your Beloved may sound easy, in actuality it takes a lot of conscious thought and effort to achieve. Not only do you have to learn how to be in a relationship with an unseen being, you also have to learn how to love the being you are in relationship with. This is the challenge of any spiritual journey. Learning how to walk a path of personal commitment to your Beloved will allow you to meet that challenge. Doing so is what will ultimately heal you forever.

Although love is a decision that you make, it is also a deep feeling. It is the feeling of love that compels us to make the decision to responsibly commit to maintaining our relationships. Without feeling love for your Beloved, your relationship will remain largely intellectual and, consequently, will not be compelling. The question is: How do you fall in love with someone that you can't see and that your ego tells you is not real? The answer is to become intellectually aware of your Beloved first, ignore your ego, and then begin grappling with the concept of learning how to communicate with them. This is what this book is for. In it, I can give you an intellectual description of your Beloved and teach you the techniques that will allow you to contact them. I cannot, however, cause you to fall in love with them. That will happen of its own accord when you are ready to receive them.

Once you are ready, they will enter and there will be nothing you can do to stop it. Preparing yourself to receive them is your goal. You do that by opening your mind to the possibility of eternal love and then by wanting it. This sounds simple, but if you haven't done it yet, there must be a few beliefs that are standing in your way that must be transformed and purified before it can occur. Therefore, ferreting out those beliefs is a prerequisite. Once you have done so, you will meet your Beloved. As a matter of fact, you will not be able to escape them. That is because, once you realize they are real, there will be no turning back. Since they are part of you, where would you turn back to?

After your Beloved becomes real to you, you must do something with them. What you do with them is dependent on your understanding of love. If all your beliefs about love are conditional, your relationship with your Beloved will be very disappointing to you. You will be disappointed because your Beloved will not enter into a conditional relationship with you. Because they are real, they have their own understanding of what a loving relationship is. The only kind of relationship they will enter into with you is a deeply committed, unconditionally loving relationship that is totally fulfilling. Although they are willing to teach you how to do this, you must commit to learning it if your relationship is to be a success. My entire healing has revolved around learning how to do this. Yours will also revolve around this learning. That is because this is how one heals their spiritual body.

Once you have learned how to create an unconditionally loving relationship with your Beloved, you will be able to align your vibration with theirs. Through the intensity of your combined desire, a special resonance of healing is created. That resonance is generally a combination of several emotions, such as love, trust, gratitude, happiness, joy, and surrender. When you achieve this resonance with your Beloved, an explosion of thought and feeling will occur, and in a very real sense, you merge with your Beloved. You feel their presence physically. It may feel like a healing wind, an electrical shock, burning heat, or a gentle embrace. Sometimes they may enter into a specific area of your body, or a specific chakra, to cleanse and purify it. This creates a pleasant, warm sensation. Whatever occurs, the experience is incredibly magical and there are no words that can adequately describe it. It is always accompanied by deep emotion that literally turns one inside out with desire and longing.

Although your Beloved can heal you instantly, it is important to remember that healing is an ongoing process. It took me years to develop an unconditionally loving relationship with my Beloved. In order to do it, I had to consciously think about love all the time. A commitment to my Beloved only came after I learned how to trust. It also came after years of doubt in which my ego constantly told me that my Beloved wasn't real. I did not feel him moving within me, as I do now, until after I had many little miracles that gradually shifted my perceptions into higher consciousness. If you do not experience instantaneous healing the first time you meet your Beloved, it doesn't mean that you are not being healed. Every time you shift your perceptions into higher consciousness by learning how to love, you are making progress toward your goal and you are in the process of healing.

It is important to be flexible about how your healing comes and also to give up control. Because belief will be lacking, many people won't be able to receive miraculous healing. Therefore, they must use another method. If they use that method in conjunction with inner work, the two together can have a miraculous effect. Even allopathic medicine can be used positively, for though it is at least in some cases the most destructive and toxic of all the alternatives, it does have the ability to buy a person time. If one uses that time to do inner work, even this method can accomplish a positive result.

Whether one's belief is lacking or not, it is important to realize that one's Beloved can heal them at any time. Sometimes it is miraculous healing that causes an unbeliever to begin their spiritual journey. Other times, miraculous healing only comes after years of inner work. There seems to be no magical formula for creating it. Only your higher consciousness knows why it is given at one time and not another. Since I have received miraculous healing several times, I do know that one's opportunities to receive it are unlimited and that the closer one is to their Beloved, the more likely it is to occur.

Healing, like everything else you do with your Beloved, is a co-creation. Although your Beloved can heal you miraculously, it is your combined love that is the key. As you desire to know them and to understand Love, you will shift your perceptions into higher consciousness, which will then activate your Beloved's voice. Once their voice is activated, they will continue to help you see things differently. Eventually, your combined love will unite into an explosion of light in which your energies will blend and mingle. Because this will create immediate, positive, miraculous change, it will heal you.

You cannot cajole, beg, or pretend your Beloved into healing you. Your Beloved knows your every thought, word, and deed from the inside out. They already know where your motivation is coming from. If it's not coming from love, it's coming from fear, and they can't unite with that because fear isn't in their vibration. If the only reason you are motivated to heal is because you're afraid of the disease you have manifested and not because you truly want to change, asking them to heal you miraculously doesn't make a lot of sense because your request will simply fall on deaf ears. Your Beloved is not an enabler. They will never come between you and your creations, for that would give you the wrong kind of message. Therefore, until you truly desire to know and embody Love, they will not be motivated to intercede for you.

When you create a loving relationship with your Beloved, you must become real, which means to become honest and authentic. As you strive to learn the truth about how you are creating your particular life circumstances through your beliefs and attitudes, you must express all of your feelings. Some of these feelings may be rage, hate, resentment, and blame. Although these are not pleasant emotions, when they come from your truth, your Beloved will accept them all with grace and unconditional love. As you are willing to become real for your Beloved, your Beloved will be willing to do the same for you by showing you just how real they are. Since Love is the only reality, by becoming real and denying nothing, you can begin to experience healing.

When this occurs, Love has no form. It is a pure experience of being that comes from total trust. It is an ability to step back so that something greater than you can lead the way. In order to do that, you must be willing to give up control and allow healing to come from within. How it comes is not up to you, but trusting that it will come, is. This is all that you must do to assure yourself a long and healthy, pain-free life that comes miraculously.

I believe that receiving healing is your divine right as a spiritual being. If healing is divine, it can only come through Love. By creating an intense, loving, and holy relationship with your Beloved, you will learn what creating a real relationship is all about. Your Beloved will become your "savior" who will lead you through the darkness of your own personal lies to the light of truth. When you are willing to allow this to unfold, you will become a spiritual adult.

Once you are able to fearlessly follow your Beloved anywhere, giving up all control, you will begin to experience the kind of love that can even heal your karmic birth defects, your chemistry and mechanics, and every disease known to man, instantly and miraculously without taking a single pill or excising a single organ. This is the kind of Love that surpasses all understanding, the Love that knows no bounds and is beyond limitation of any kind.

Chapter 6

Shedding Light on Inner Voices

A successful person is personally powerful, for they have learned that no one can hurt them but themselves. Their desire for authenticity and depth allows them to become an honest person who takes responsibility for the reality they create through their beliefs, without blaming that reality on others. Although the accumulation of physical abundance usually follows the personally powerful, wealth and status are not necessarily part of this definition of success. Rather, success is internal, having to do with how close, intimate, and caring one has become with their spiritual nature, the part of themselves that has an evolved character with high ideals, as well as the hope, courage, and commitment to do the right thing, even though it may not be convenient.

In order to align your consciousness with your spiritual nature, you must listen to the stories you tell yourself. Within your consciousness is a committee filled with many inner characters who can be imaginatively conceptualized in form. Your Beloved's voice is only one voice among many. Because it is a still, small voice, if you do not focus your attention on hearing it, the other voices that speak louder will drown it out. Your Beloved's voice will always motivate you to behave in accordance with your spiritual nature. People who haven't yet made the decision to become personally powerful simply won't hear it. That is because hearing the Beloved's voice is a conscious decision one makes.

Why is it a time-consuming process to learn how to hear your Beloved's voice? It is because of all the erroneous beliefs you have been programmed with. Your Beloved will only tell you the truth, yet if you don't know what the truth is, it will be impossible to hear what they have to say. In order to do so, you must become aware of the kinds of things they will tell you. Then, when you "hear" them tell you something else, you will know immediately that another one of your inner characters is masquerading as your Beloved and is speaking in their place.

So, what is the truth? In my opinion, your Beloved will always tell you that they love you now and have always loved you despite any errors of judgment you have made in the past or will make in the future. They also want you to succeed and be happy by giving you everything your heart desires. However, since they are limited by your beliefs, they can't give you your heart's desires until you consciously choose to change the beliefs that prevent their creation. They will tell you that they can help you learn the lessons that you, yourself, decided you needed to learn in this incarnation. Once you do, all your pain will end. They will not come between you and your creations, but they will intercede for you when you are truly ready to change by finding a better way.

Your Beloved will also tell you that you have many strengths, powers, and talents that lie dormant within you. Once you resonate with them and learn how to manifest them physically, the strengths, powers, and talents will become the magnet that will attract a successful, abundant external reality to you.

Your Beloved can help you find these strengths, powers, and talents and will provide you with the opportunities to use them positively to create healing for yourself and others. It is through healing that a channel for their love, in the form of physical health and abundance, enters into you. This is how they can help you transform your entire life into peace and joy.

If you have not been taught to believe these things, you won't allow your Beloved to say them to you, and you certainly won't act as if they are true. Without believing them, you will blame your reality of pain on external influences. Through blame, you will rationalize your desire to dominate, manipulate, and control. By behaving in an unloving way, you will hurt yourself. The hurt creates pain which must be numbed through addictions. Slowly, your reality will disintegrate into ill health; conflict; mental, emotional, and/or financial poverty; and disaster. Without finding the strengths, powers, and talents that lie dormant within you, you will live a mediocre life in which all your energy is given over to creating somebody else's dream.

Why do you want to learn how to hear your Beloved's voice? It is simply because theirs is the voice of Truth that will motivate you into turning your dormant potential into positive, miraculous achievement. All your other inner voices will simply lead you astray while they create a meaningless reality filled with inner pain.

In order to hear your Beloved's voice, it is a good idea to become consciously aware of the kinds of things your other voices are likely to say. Then, when you hear your Beloved say them, you will be aware that someone else is masquerading in their place. Your inner characters advocate specific categories of belief. By personifying them in form, you can talk to them about what they believe and why they believe it. You can then get a sense of the feelings these beliefs are likely to generate. Besides motivating behavior, feelings also create resonance, which is attractive. Ultimately, it is the beliefs of your inner characters that will create your entire reality. Your healing resides in transforming their beliefs into positive, productive ones that promote health and well-being.

In this chapter I'll discuss a few of the most common inner characters, emphasizing their negative beliefs. In the following chapter I will discuss how to transform their negative beliefs into the positive ones that your Beloved can use to heal you. As you read through the list, try to recognize which inner characters play the greatest role in your life.

The inner judge, also sometimes known as your critical parent, is full of dogma. They want you to conform to external, socially acceptable rules. They are perfectionistic, overly critical, and punitive. They have rules about everything. They like to browbeat you into obeying their rules. They want you to pay for every mistake and misdemeanor you make with guilt and are glad when you suffer for your errors. "Should" is their favorite word, and they think you need their authoritative words to keep yourself in line. Besides being punitive and perfectionistic, they are self-righteous and rigid in their judgments. Some of you may recognize this voice as a major part of your psyche because it is one few people can escape.

The voice of the inner priest — also known as the inner guru, nun, monk, and true believer — is the voice most easily confused with your Beloved. It can spout the dogma of any religion or spiritual persuasion or it can be atheistic in nature. Its rhetoric is based on whatever it believes will be your pathway to salvation.

That pathway can be herbs, vitamins, and exercise, as well as money or worship. Although this voice may not spout religious dogma, it is still a "true believer" in whatever it believes. Consequently, everyone has one whether they are religious or not.

The inner priest's voice will usually be the one who talks to you about morality, values, and principles. It will tell you that anyone who does not believe as you do is wrong, or perhaps even "sinful," if this is a word it has in its vocabulary. In this respect, it is a judgmental voice filled with self-righteous blame. When you listen to its voice, you will see yourself as justified in attacking others. The voice of the inner priest teaches you to believe that exoneration will someday come to you either on the judgment day when your enemies (everyone who doesn't believe as you do) will be cast into hell and you won't, or, in the future, as history proves you right and all the non-believers wrong.

Another inner voice that can be very harmful is your inner cynic. Listening to their voice will make you depressed and will resign you to failure. They are often apathetic, causing you to be inactive and unmotivated. They search for the flaws in everything and are happy when they find them. They are the voice that warns you not to be "too happy" for something bad is bound to happen sooner or later. The cynic uses doubt to maintain a false position of power. It makes them feel good to prove others wrong or less intelligent than they. They are frequently atheistic and are often quite paranoid, unconsciously believing that their cynicism keeps them safe from failure. Unfortunately, it also keeps them safe from open-minded exploration as well. The voice of the cynic is a good one to be aware of. This voice can keep you from ever meeting your Beloved because it will tell you that you can never be sure of whose voice you are hearing, so why bother. And isn't it all just useless fantasy anyway? The inner cynic can be persuasive, forceful, and intelligent.

Mr. or Ms. Together is another good voice to know about. They are calm, cool, and collected. They have life all sewn up. They don't believe they need to do any inner work because they don't have any problems. For them, denial is the name of the game, and although they can perceive other people's problems, they believe that they themselves are totally "together." They are generally superficial, which means they are without the depth it takes to really look within and perceive the pain and heartache that is there. They live life on the surface and believe that if they can keep up the right appearances, they will be a success. Mr. or Ms. Together performs life but they never really live it.

The inner king or queen is the part of you that is a tyrant. They are arrogant and want to be given credit where credit is due and, in their opinion, it is always due to them. They like to be in control and want to have their own way. They tend to be dictatorial and misuse their power. People who have a strong inner king or queen are thought of as being bossy and uncaring. They tend to make poor listeners and have inflated egos. They are also pompous, superior, and condescending towards others, especially anyone who might display perceived weaknesses. They are the type of people who like to lead others but they do it in such a way that they foster either allies or enemies, neither of which are friends.

The unhealed inner child is the part of you that is insecure and needy. They are generally helpless and completely dependent on someone else to take care of them. They have enormous issues around abandonment. To them, abandonment means sudden death, which terrifies them. Consequently, they also feel very vulnerable and can become manipulative because of it. The hallmark of the unhealed inner child is that they are self-centered, self-indulgent, and narcissistic. They can be quite demanding when it comes to getting their own way. They generally lack self-discipline and do not take responsibility for the consequences of their actions. They tend to whine a lot and are easily frightened by inconsequential fears that others must protect them from.

The hallmark of the unhealed inner adolescent is that they are self-important. Although they have figured out that the world doesn't revolve around them, they still think their wants, needs, and desires are more important than anyone else's. They tend to be their own worst enemies and live their lives by absolutes which they believe bring order to the chaos of their lives. Your unhealed inner adolescent is the part of you that believes you'll never be happy, be a success, or get what you want. They have big "deservingness" issues and try to inflate their egos by aggrandizing their bodies. To the unhealed inner adolescent, the body beautiful is all important and it must be primped and decorated for all occasions. Because they are form-conscious and haven't yet realized that beauty is found within, they spend a great deal of time doing activities that will either enhance their beauty or increase their sexual desirability. This behavior is fostered by insecurity, which they deal with by becoming either arrogant or self-deprecating — two sides of the same coin. They have many faces and, as you explore your psyche, you may find that the unhealed inner adolescent plays a major role.

An aspect of the inner adolescent that can be put into its own separate category is the rebel. This is the voice in you that says it is going to do whatever it damn well pleases no matter what anyone else says. This is also the voice that caused you to start smoking cigarettes, take drugs, drive fast cars, become promiscuous, or do any of the other wild and crazy things you did when you were a teenager or young adult. The rebel is usually stubborn and hard-headed and inconsiderate of others. They tend to be reckless and self-destructive. Although the rebel's voice becomes quieter as you age, in its heyday it can cause you quite a lot of harm.

The inner adventurer is that part of you that enjoys being a rolling stone and having no commitments. People who have a strong inner adventurer like to be wanderers, without care or responsibility. They tend to be shallow and need excitement so they can feel alive. They are always looking for the pot of gold at the end of the rainbow that is just around the next bend. They have little perseverance and wander from place to place and job to job. If they have families, they often drag them around with them, subjecting them to the rootlessness of their lives.

The inner warrior is a destroyer — violent, ruthless, and destructive. The warrior in you worships conflict and competition. Its basic drive in life is to achieve by winning at all costs, without caring how it is done. To your warrior, the end justifies the means. A person with a strong inner warrior is usually overbalanced in male energy, believing in the power of domination, manipulation, and control.

The inner romantic exemplifies the side of you that is over-balanced in female energy. This voice tends to be overly emotional and clinging. The inner romantic belies that others should take care of them. They can also be possessive, jealous and quite blind when it comes to reason. As they look at the object of their desire through the passion of love, they can be totally illogical when it comes to making decisions that require some rational thought.

The inner rescuer likes to take care of people. Rescuers are always looking for victims to care for and smother in love. They deny their own needs in favor of self-sacrifice which, for them, is a form of control. They can become terribly hurt and manipulative when the person they are sacrificing for is unappreciative. Their hidden agenda is to evoke guilt in the person being rescued so that they will be faithful to the rescuer for life. By making their victim dependent on what the rescuer does for them, the rescuer finally feels safe.

The inner victim is the part of you that sees yourself as weak and helpless. This inner voice is always telling you how dependent you are and how unable you are to help yourself by changing the situation. People with a strong inner victim are frequently sick but take no responsibility for their own healing. They are in constant blame but they never do anything about the wrongs they think are being heaped upon them. They are the "poor me" types, powerless, paranoid, and filled with self-pity. They are long suffering, lonely, depressed, feeling desperate, and hopeless about their situation. For some reason, they can never figure any way out of their problems. The hallmark of a victim is that they always blame others for their problems and never take responsibility for having created them.

The voice of the inner bully is just the opposite. The bully's voice seeks revenge. Someone with a strong inner bully likes to make other people pay for the mistakes they've made. Since they hold everyone else responsible for their troubles, they are also great blamers. However, they are out for blood, seeing themselves as justified in putting people in their place. As a result, they tend to be abusive, vengeful, and punishing people who justify their punishment by believing it has a righteous cause.

93

The voice of the martyr consists of the victim, rescuer, and bully simultaneously. Therefore, the martyr's face is always shifting and changing as it takes on different and seemingly opposed roles. For this reason, the psyche of the martyr can be a difficult one to understand, as it is filled with inconsistencies — one minute they are the victim, the next a persecutor who wants to make others pay for what they've done, and the next a rescuer who is out to save the world. The martyr is frequently full of self-pity and self-right-eous blame. They hold others responsible for the failures in their life and are filled with grievances. This makes them feel justified in their abuse. This abuse is often passive-aggressive, so that no one can accuse them of being a bully. The hallmark of the martyr is that they are always innocent and believe that they, themselves, are beyond all blame. It is important to become intimate with the martyr's voice since few people are able to escape its influence.

In addition to the above-mentioned inner characters that promote certain beliefs, we also have inner voices that promote specific feelings. These are the emotional inner voices. There are two broad categories of these voices — the *voice of love* and the *voice of fear*. In the *voice of love* are all the emotions we have traditionally called positive because they make us feel good. In the *voice of fear* are all the emotions we have traditionally called negative because they make us feel bad. The emotions in the *voice of fear* are all con-tracting, because they motivate us to withdraw or "shrink" by caus-ing us to believe in the probability of failure. The emotions in the *voice of love* are all expansive, because they motivate us to expand or "stand out" by causing us to believe in the probability of success.

It is the *voice of love* that everyone needs to have and allow themselves to hear if they are to heal. When this inner voice is allowed to speak to you and you give yourself permission to hear it and be moved by it, your inner healing will progress at a much faster rate. I doubt that one could heal at all if they weren't in contact with this voice.

It is the *voice of love* that I have personified as the Beloved. Everyone has this inner voice within them but it often lies dormant for most of one's lifetime. It is the voice of unconditional love and it can heal all things by its love. It heals you by allowing you to be whatever you are or to have whatever feelings you are feeling. It never tells you that you need to be different than you are, but it does encourage you to be all that you can be. This voice longs to be one with you and to be the only voice you ever hear. It is the voice of simple wisdom that knows that, if you are to improve yourself, you must first be loved the way you are.

The *voice of love* never speaks loudly, shouts, or cajoles. It knows that you must be left to make your own decisions and to make your own mistakes. It is always there, however, waiting for you to notice its quiet whispers. The *voice of love* is always soft. It has no rough edges. It knows that for you to hear it, you must freely choose it. In this way, love will flower between you and that which it represents so that you can heal. It longs to bring you joy, peace, and bliss, but it will never force this on you for joy, peace, and bliss must also be freely chosen before they can be received. This is the voice of all good things — love, hope, faith, and charity — and when you listen to it you will never be deceived.

This is also the voice that your Beloved embodies. As you see your Beloved in form, they will be all things to you that you want them to be. If it's a soft and gentle mother that you need to have, hold, and rock you, they will be that. If it's a strong, protecting father that you need to keep you safe and secure, they will be that. If it's a lover you need, longing to cover you with kisses, inflame you with passion, hold you close, and never let you go, they will be that. If it's a wise and caring guide or compassionate friend you need, they will be that. You can either separate these aspects of your Beloved into separate forms or roll them all into one. They are content to do and be whatever you want them to do and be as long as it is unconditionally loving. However, if you want them to be angry, condemning, judgmental, cynical, irresponsible, punishing, falsely pious, needy, blaming, or rebellious, you will be talking to someone else, and even though they may wear the face and form of your Beloved in your visualization, it won't really be them.

Like all our other inner voices, the emotional voices are also always speaking to us. Depending on how you are feeling about yourself, they either speak to you with the voice of love or the voice of fear. Since the voice of love speaks softest, when you are in the midst of an identity crisis, you will probably be feeling the effects of the voice of fear instead. These voices are always detrimental, for they motivate non-productive behavior, as well as create a resonance that attracts pain. The voice of fear has seven root emotions that most characterize its energy. These root emotions are shame, anger, hurt, despair, hopelessness, fear, and loneliness. Although everyone feels them all to different degrees at some time in their life, each person has a favored one that speaks louder to them than all the rest. As I list them, note the one that speaks loudest in you.

Shame has several components. They are denial, self-hatred, undeservingness, and guilt. The aspect of shame that is denial will tell you that you have never had, now or in the past, any redeeming qualities. Because it denies you your strengths, powers, and talents, it keeps you in a state of paralysis so that you cannot improve yourself. It calls you stupid and refuses to believe you have the intelligence to figure out how to go about healing yourself. It tells you that you don't know enough, haven't learned enough, don't have the right degrees or credentials or whatever it is that you believe should provide you with a hard-earned ticket for success.

The aspect of shame that speaks for self-hatred is extremely destructive. It tells you that you are wrong and bad no matter what you do, and it is glad when you fail so it can say, "I told you so!" It is very similar in nature to the part of shame that speaks for undeservingness, which will stop you dead in your tracks when it comes to creating something you desire, just for the fun of it. It will even tell you that you are undeserving of having your needs fulfilled and that you'd better be satisfied with what you've got. This is the aspect of shame that comes up with all kinds of lame excuses for why you shouldn't have the reality you want.

Shame is also a guilty voice. For this reason, it is a particularly insidious one. It holds you responsible for all the sins of the world. People who feel a lot of shame often immerse themselves in guilt. They do not need to be told they create their own reality. They have always known that, because of their inner flaws, they are the cause of all their problems. Their guilt causes them to writhe in self-hatred, which has absolutely no redeeming qualities whatsoever.

Anger is another root emotion in the voice of fear that speaks very loudly in some people. Anger is often the result of a sudden or extreme loss of power. People who use this voice often feel deprived. A loss of self or soul can trigger it. Anger can seethe in silence or be very loud. It can be demonstrative and wordy or quiet and slow. It can be directed outward at other people or inward toward the self. The voice of anger can be very compelling and can cause you to do or say things that you will later regret. The behavior that it motivates is socially unappealing and is, therefore, probably the most repressed of the root emotions. It can, however, be a tremendous force for good, especially when it is expressed appropriately to create positive change.

You may have a very loud inner voice that talks to you about hurt, despair, or hopelessness. These contracting emotions are similar but not quite the same. A person who feels hopeless feels powerless to overcome their burdens. Their problems seem just too heavy to bear. It is a crushing emotion that destroys one's motivation to change. People who have it as their root emotion feel overpowered by the weight of the world. Hopelessness will cause you to give up your journey to your Beloved before it has even begun, and despair will cause you to abandon the journey at the first sign of distress.

Despair is a howling emotion. It feels massive pain. People who are despairing become despondent and depressed, not wanting to get out of bed in the morning, wanting just to cover their heads and cry from the depths of their agony. They have lost all of their motivation to succeed and will give up before they have even begun. After all, what's the use of trying if they are only going to fail?

The voice of hurt is acutely aware of the pain it feels. It feels hurt by everyone and everything and is paralyzed by it. People who have this as their root emotion take offense at every slight and even imagine offenses when none were intended. It's almost as if they look for reasons to feel hurt by others. They tend to make themselves more important than they are, thinking that others are out to hurt them and do them wrong. They are extremely sensitive to criticism and they are the type of person that one must be delicate with in order to keep from hurting their feelings.

The emotion of fear itself has its own unique voice. It is one of the most destructive root emotions and it speaks very loudly. For some, it will control every aspect of their life. Fear needs no excuses to exist and flies in the face of all reason. The words it likes to use best are, "What if ... " Then it scares you to death by parading every macabre scene of pain and failure before your eyes in order to paralyze you. People who have fear as their root emotion are terrified of change because change produces the big unknown. To them, stepping into the void is tantamount to utter stupidity. Fear is the biggest block many people have to achieving success on their spiritual journey because it stops them from ever even taking the first step. The emotion of fear speaks loudest when it is aligned with loneliness.

People whose root emotion is loneliness believe that they are all alone and always will be. Even though they may have a spouse or external lover, they deny that this person can ever really know them. And, worse than that, they are in denial of their Beloveds, proclaiming that anything beyond their five senses (touching, tasting, smelling, seeing, or hearing) exists only in the realm of their imagination and is nothing more than a fantasy. They deny that any help could ever be given to them by the divine and believe that there are no such things as angels, guides, or unseen friends. These people are lonely indeed and, though they may be wandering in the wilderness, they never stumble upon the promised land of love for which they constantly search but never find.

You may discover other root emotions in the voice of fear as you do your own inner work. The ones I have described will at least help you be aware of what to look for and how to proceed.

Some of the emotions which fall into the category of the *voice of love* are happiness, joy, peace, trust, hope, optimism, gratitude, and love. I am going to attempt to define them for you. However, since they are continuously expanding, evolving, and growing emotions, it's hard to contain them in words, which are limiting forms.

Happiness is a state of contentment. It results when all our needs are fulfilled. Therefore, when we feel happy, we are without worry or fear. Joy, on the other hand, is the fulfillment of our preferences. Joy is when you've found your life's purpose and are living it all the time as an integral, living, breathing part of your life, which is utterly fulfilling.

Through the fulfillment of happiness and joy comes peace, which is a state of calm, quiet, and tranquility. Peace is more than just the absence of strife. It is a quiet knowing that comes from having an operating knowledge of reality creation and feeling totally bathed in divine and eternal Love. Peace is an emotion of total safety that comes from perfect trust.

Trust rests on sound, provable metaphysical principles that work. Trust is self-reliance. It is the faith you have in yourself, that you will be able to understand your lessons when they come, that you will own your personal mistakes that need to be owned, and change when you need to change. Trust also comes when you have the ability to receive guidance through inner listening, knowing that you will be shown the way.

Trust goes hand in hand with hope. When a person allows their life to unfold, experience by experience, as they follow their heart's desire, they are in a place of enormous trust and unwarranted hope. Hope is seeing the future as if it were alive with possibilities. It is a feeling that what is wanted will happen even though they don't know how it will manifest. Therefore, it is an anticipation or expectation of total joy.

Optimism is the ability to always expect the best outcome in any circumstance. Although optimism recognizes lessons that must be learned, an optimistic person uses their lessons to further their growth, knowing that, as they evolve their consciousness, the good in every situation will be understood and, thus, received. An optimistic person is willing to see the world as a friendly place with lessons to give as gifts that will propel them on their way.

Gratitude is the result of right thinking. It is a deep feeling of thankfulness for gifts of Love that have been received. True gratitude can only be felt when a person recognizes their own divinity, which means they simultaneously recognize everyone else's as well. Gratitude comes from knowing that you have been given everything, and, since you are a creator, you can learn how to responsibly receive it. Gratitude goes hand in hand with love because you can only feel grateful for what you love.

Now I will attempt to define the ultimate paradox, which is love itself. Earlier I defined love as an illusive quality of being that takes great wisdom to achieve. Love is both male and female, being created out of thought and feeling. It is, first and foremost, a deeply felt and intense emotion that can't accurately be described. It can only be experienced. Out of this experience we call love is born a deep, unfailing commitment that is beyond all logic and reason. This commitment breeds a desire to responsibly maintain the relationship so that more feelings of love can be created. The quality of being we call love is the feminine principle, the original energy out of which all things came. It is the feminine energy that gives birth to the masculine, which is that of action and commitment and responsibility, so that, together, the two of them can create all that is good and desirable. When one begins to experience this kind of love for their Beloved, they will hold the key to reality creation, and it is this key that will unlock the treasure house of heaven, which will shower them with eternal bliss.

These are just some of the expanding emotions that are contained within the voice of love. When you have them in great abundance, they produce a resonance that can only attract success. When you make a conscious decision to hear Love's voice, you will heal. Once you make this decision, your Beloved will become the guide who will teach you how to heal every aspect of your reality.

Chapter 7

Transformation

In actuality, your many inner characters who voice limited beliefs aren't bad in and of themselves. They have simply been perverted into negative caricatures of what they were really meant to be. If understood correctly, each of the voices can be directed toward keeping you safe and loved in the way you were meant to be kept safe and loved. The task, then, is not to rid yourself of the voices, which is impossible, but to unite them into one voice, the *voice of Love*, as personified by your Beloved. This is done by attributing to each voice a higher purpose. When your purpose is to understand reality creation by balancing your thoughts and feelings in the heart, each of the voices will take on a new energy that will propel you in a totally different direction than the dark and painful one it sent you in before.

In order to heal your inner characters, they must be re-educated. Since your inner characters have always existed to keep you safe, when you redefine what safety is, their attitudes will change immediately. These new attitudes will, in turn, cause them to redefine what it is they want for you. As you align all of your inner voices into a single purpose, you reduce and eventually eliminate your inner conflicts that create the static that prevents you from hearing the *voice of Love* and reaching your goal.

This static results in reduced or sporadic motivation. Because our inner conflicts confuse us, they retard our ability to reach a level of undivided motivation, otherwise known as a single purpose and a solitary intent. There is no more powerful force in the universe than a single purpose and a solitary intent. When you have a single, unequivocal intent to heal, you will do whatever it is your inner voices direct you to do. When all your inner voices are knowledgeable and wise because you have consciously evolved their under-standing of reality creation, your progress along the path will be steady and sure. A single force of energy is then created which will propel you along the way. As you learn to discern the truth about how you are creating your reality, erroneous beliefs will fall by the wayside. You will be carried along, as if on a tidal wave of power, that will deposit you at the very foot of all that you desire.

I believe that healing comes from knowing that you create your own reality. When your attitude motivates you to transform limiting beliefs that create a non-productive reality, you will have developed the right attitude for success. This attitude will motivate you to figure out how you are creating your reality. It will cause you to take a long, hard look at what you've been taught to believe and at the feelings those beliefs have generated. It will help you to understand why you think what you think and why you do what you do. You will also develop personal techniques for further healing and you will know that, in the final analysis, your healing rests on your shoulders. Knowing that you are responsible for creating your own reality is tremendously exciting and freeing, because you will now be motivated to live a life filled with wonderful inner discoveries that will teach you how to be wise.

When you proceed to heal the attitude of your inner characters, you must first define clearly for yourself what it means to heal. If you should decide that ultimate healing is reached by knowing and understanding Love, you will develop a plan of action based on achieving this. For example, if you want to begin to learn about Love by developing a relationship with your Beloved, you will consciously devise an external plan of action with this as the goal. That external plan may be to meditate with your Beloved a specific number of times per week and to have that meditation include certain activities and to focus on specific topics.

You may also want your external plan to include saying an ever-expanding and evolving set of affirmations on a regular basis. It may include starting a journal or doing some other kind of creative work that serves to focus your attention inward. It may mean developing a relationship with your inner child and adolescent and deciding to do inner rescue work on a regular basis. It could include taking workshops and seminars or going to metaphysical bookstores and buying books on the subject of healing that appeal to you. It may mean exploring, with an open mind, a variety of churches or different spiritual paths to see what kind of direction they can give you. As you begin exploring what it means to be spiritual by whatever means makes the most sense to you, you can begin the process of healing.

On the other hand, your external plan may not include any of these things because these activities just don't appeal to you. In that case, you must create a different kind of plan, one that does appeal to you. Whatever you decide, it is important that your plan include some conscious way of exploring the concepts of conscious reality creation I have been describing here. If it does not, you will continue to run your life by past concepts that have not served you beneficially.

If you do not like the concept of working with the Beloved, it is still important that you learn how to contact the *voice of love*. Knowing that resonance has drawn you to your present reality, including your diseases, accidents of fate, conflicts, and financial circumstances, you must become an authentic human being who is willing to own and transform the beliefs that got you here. I believe that as you become emotionally honest with yourself and work with your conscience, you will contact this voice whether you personify it as the Beloved or not.

If your tastes are more esoteric than I have described so far in this book, you might want your external plan of action to include energy work or work with crystals as tools for focusing energy, doing breathing techniques, or saying mantras that you have borrowed from Eastern religions or made up yourself. You might want to get thoroughly involved in Native American rituals that honor all living things or work with Egyptian or other mystery schools that deal with color and sound as healing modalities. There are many traditions that are more aligned with the Goddess religion that you might want to explore, such as Paganism. You could choose to focus your attention on the teachings of an inspirational healer, such as Jesus or Lazaris, or someone else who thoroughly knows the basics of reality creation. The point is to begin your search somewhere by beginning to explore what is available to you with an open mind. Although most religious traditions have been polluted by erroneous, limited beliefs simply because they haven't understood true reality creation, you can still explore them if you keep in mind that you need not throw out the baby with the bath water. The truth in them is still there for the finding.

If you are unfamiliar with any of the spiritual paths I have mentioned, they are all worth exploring. Most of them will not be what you think they are. I have explored many of them and I can honestly say that I have never gone into a church or participated in another spiritual tradition I didn't like. That is because each one of them contains at least a portion of the truth and each leads to Love in their own unique way. As long as I left my spiritual arrogance at the door and entered with an open mind, I received guidance in the form of insights and new ideas everywhere I went.

Whatever you decide, the point is to create an external plan of some kind which is both solid and fluid. In this way you create boundaries for yourself and as the river flows and changes its direction, so can you. An external plan gives you something to get started with, as well as some kind of routine to live your life by. It gives you principles to adhere to — something spiritual to focus your attention on.

After you've created this plan, you need to dialogue with all your inner characters and make a new contract with them. In this new contract, they will be enlisted as aides that will help you fulfill your external plan for healing. You can do this in the trance state by personifying the characters in form, or you can write it in your journal. You can even act it out if that is a method that appeals to you. The object is not to suppress the voices of your inner characters, but to re-educate them to see if the two of you, working together, can come up with a plan that will keep you on the right path doing the right thing.

If any of your inner characters have extreme objections to the external plan of action you have created, find out why by letting them talk. If you don't find out what their objections are and deal with these objections realistically, they will sabotage every effort you make toward healing.

Once they are re-educated, their objections will probably be reasonable enough. Because they know you are willing to hear them, they won't be judgmental, rebellious, cynical, or shallow anymore. Rather, they will make valuable suggestions that can help you to re-evaluate your plan to make it more realistic for you. Because of their suggestions, you might find you've bitten off more than you can chew or that the plan doesn't fit well with your personality. When you have looked your plan over from all angles by working with each of your inner characters, you can come up with something that all your inner characters will approve of. Aligning your inner voices will do much to propel you speedily on your way.

Once you re-educate your inner characters, the voice of your judge won't need to be condemning or punitive anymore. Because your judge is now educated as to the uselessness and foolishness of their action, they will know it is an inappropriate means of control to use. However, because they know their voice is needed, they can gently remind you to stay on task with your new plan of action and tell you the reasons why. They can help you find ways to modify the current plan if it's not working. They can help you with discrimination and discernment as you do your exploration of the different spiritual paths that are available to you. Your judge can be a powerful motivator when their voice is aligned with truth and balanced by love.

The judge is also very practical. They know when you are getting too "airy fairy," too lazy, or too unbalanced. When re-educated, they know that all four bodies need to be aligned and that none of them should be ignored. Therefore, if you are becoming too solitary as you do your spiritual work, they may remind you to go play and have fun. However, they will also be the ones to remind you to buckle down if you go too long without doing any inner work. Therefore, they can help you to prioritize your activities so that you can create the time and space to do what you need to do. They can show you the way to integrity and how to be true to your goals. These are all excellent jobs for the judge that are beneficial to you instead of harmful.

The re-educated inner priest is a very important inner character to have. The priest can keep you forever searching for the light because they know it can be found. They are curious about all things esoteric and have an unquenchable thirst for the divine. They are in touch with that part of you that longs to be spiritual. They can help you evoke this desire if you are not in touch with it already. They are the ones who thirst for more understanding, more love, more divinity, more truth. They are strongly committed, and, when that commitment has high ideals filled with right thought that propel you in a right direction, their aid is invaluable. Therefore, working with and re-educating your inner priest is a very important aspect of your inner healing.

Even a cynic has redeeming qualities if you turn your cynic into a skeptic. A skeptic is highly protective of you. They will cause you to examine every thought to find the truth in it. They will not allow you to believe in every book you read or every spiritual leader you hear. However, a healthy skeptic is open-minded enough to examine the facts and try out new ideas if they seem acceptable. Skeptics can allow themselves to grapple with the unknown until it proves itself one way or another. They can help you gather facts and do research on different spiritual paths and their positive benefits. Skeptics are very important people to have around because they, too, are discerning.

Mr. or Ms. Together also has many redeeming qualities when re-educated. They are the most practical ones of all for keeping you safe on the physical plane. They are full of self-confidence and know they can get you out of any troubles that might befall you while you are on your spiritual journey. They know they can learn to understand reality creation if given enough time and, when they do, they can use that information to do awesome and wonderful things. When Mr. or Ms. Together has depth, there is no end to what they can create with their self-confidence.

Your inner king or queen is a necessary part of your personality and is essential as you become successful. They are born leaders and know how to take charge. They are good organizers who know how to delegate authority to others. They are also noble and self-confident and have a sense of presence and deservingness. They appreciate luxury and the finer things in life and don't find it a disgrace to lovingly indulge themselves in it. When re-educated, they are also generous and wise and are always kind to others, giving charity to all. They realize that they have a personal gift of assertiveness that allows them to protect the weak or those who are less capable than they. They use this gift wisely to bring benefit to everyone.

The healed inner child is important as well. When operating in their negative polarity, they are willful and selfish. When operating in their positive polarity, however, they are innocent, trusting, and all but divine. They are the part of you that believes in magic and knows that fairies, elves, and unseen friends are real. They are playful and unashamed of their creativity and outrageous fantasies. They love to laugh and have fun, so they are the part of you that can be the most innocently joyous. To be innocent means to be non-condemning and non-judgmental. Therefore, an innocent person is earthy, wild, and free. It is their openness to explore and experience that makes them a truly invaluable part of your personality.

Your healed inner adolescent also has redeeming qualities.

They too are still open to exploration. They delight in the new and unexpected and are curious about all things. Because they have not, as yet, become jaded, they enjoy new experiences and can be endlessly creative. They are also in touch with an inner power which is very magical.

The re-educated inner rebel is another necessary aspect of your inner self. After all, if you are not in touch with your inner rebel, how can you break away from the consensus reality and be free? A rebel can help you get angry at the lies you have been taught by the media all your life. It can cause you to get angry at the dark side of allopathic medicine. It can cause you to get angry at prejudice and what it has induced you and others to do. Anger is a tremendously impacting emotion. When you are in touch with your anger about the lies you have been taught, you will be motivated to do something about it. Now you can choose not to believe those lies anymore and to go your own way, even though there may be those in your external reality who don't want you to. If you allow your rebel to be an innovative, pioneering crusader, you will have found an extraordinarily valuable ally.

Your inner adventurer is also important when operating in their positive polarity. They are the part of you that is curious and seeks the unknown. They can be strong, energetic, and capable as they set off on their voyage of discovery. They are the part of you that loves to learn and to experience new things. When it is an inner journey of self-discovery they take, their endurance and ability to explore are greatly appreciated.

Your re-educated inner warrior is fearless and brave when working in their positive polarity. They are also down-to-earth and practical. They want to get the job done but in a logical and rational way. They are very strong in their commitment and have a sense of discipline and self-control that will remove all barriers, which are the very qualities you need to have in order to make your spiritual journey a success. Your inner warrior is also a great strategist. When working in conjunction with your re-educated inner judge, they will move you from sickness to health, simply because of their indomitable will to succeed.

Your healed inner romantic is very important when it comes to creating a relationship with your Beloved. Your inner romantic is passionate and devoted and longs for the kind of relationship only their Beloved can give them. They crave intimacy, love, and caring that has depth and authenticity. Because of their desire for this, they are willing to create the depth to find it. Your inner romantic is also sensitive, both to their own needs and to the needs of others. Therefore, they have an innate ability to give and to receive. Because they appreciate the beauty, the poetry, and the romance of love, they seek to make living their lives in a loving way a goal, a high ideal to be achieved.

It seems impossible that the rescuer, victim, and bully could have any redeeming qualities, but they do. When your inner rescuer learns their new job is to rescue you, there will be no stopping them. Enlist them to be in the service of your inner child and adolescent. They will know precisely how to keep you on task when it comes to rescuing them from their pain. They will hear no nonsense from you about not needing to care for them. They will go to bat for your inner child and adolescent every time. Watch out when the inner rescuer comes along. They like to take care of people, and when it's you they are taking care of, they will do so with a finesse that few of the other inner characters can achieve.

The inner victim, seemingly with no redeeming qualities, is a very important part of your psyche because they have the one quality that is essential to finding success on the spiritual path. That quality is helplessness. In other words, they know they need help.

When they can finally turn to their Beloved for help, they are the ones who are capable of totally surrendering to the divine. Once they do, they will be eager to seek guidance from a higher power who can give them a strong shoulder to lean on and a gentle embrace to comfort them. When they are in touch with their ability to ask for help and they ask it of their Beloved, they will receive guidance and healing every time.

Turning your inner bully into a protector is the best way to re-educate them. Let them help you draw boundaries in order to protect yourself. They will help you set the limits on what you can or cannot do, or on what others can ask of you. They can protect you from outside influences as you go within to do your inner work. Let them be the ones to say no to overwork and stress. When you hear their assertive voice telling you to take the time to heal yourself, their voice is a hard one not to obey.

As you re-educate all of your inner characters, they all become different aspects of the *voice of love.* This is the way they can be educated to heal you and not to harm you. Their change of attitude will motivate you to do what you need to do to heal. They can keep you on task by motivating you to stick to the external plan for healing you have devised. Your judge and skeptic can cause you to re-evaluate that plan periodically, and your rebel can cause you to enjoy doing your inner work by finding creative, innovative ways to heal yourself. All your inner characters will become your friends, instead of your enemies, and will heal you with their love.

The emotions categorized in the *voice of fear* are another matter altogether. Each of their voices is also designed to keep you safe, but they do this by making you afraid. You can only modify their influence by thoroughly understanding the dynamics each emotion rests on. No emotion should be suppressed, no matter how detrimental it seems to be. However, these emotions need to be transformed through understanding and love. Now that you know your life has a higher purpose and that you are not alone, you can learn how to rise above these detrimental root emotions by expressing them and using their energy to create a powerful transformative force for good. That's the only thing that seems to work for me, anyway, and the deeper I go into healing, the softer their voices become.

Rising above the *voice of fear* means knowing that the root emotions are just different aspects of fear talking to you and that they come from the identities of your past. The past was when you thought you were alone, without a Beloved to guide you home. The past was when you had all those failures because you listened to inner voices that crippled you. The past was when you didn't know the whole truth about who you really are. Now that you have truth on your side, you may still make mistakes but you will never again be a failure. That is because, ultimately, no one can fail who seeks to reach the truth.

When these voices are talking to me, I first express them and then detach myself and become wise. I know that, eventually, my mood will pass and that the pendulum will swing back in the other direction. Sometimes I actually meditatively see my consciousness rising above my body. From this higher level, I can look down on myself and be compassionate as I see how I'm suffering and hurting as the voice of fear talks to me. From this vantage point, I can begin to see all things differently. As this is occurring, I mentally send myself love, care, and comfort. I know that since I have set an unequivocal intent to heal, eventually those voices will run out of energy and it will be the voice of love that I will hear instead. As I prove to myself over and over again that there is nothing to fear from the unknown, I believe that eventually these voices will leave me for good. What I find happening is that the deeper I go into my healing, my highs become higher and last longer and my lows aren't quite so low while the voices aren't so vicious and they run out of rhetoric much more quickly than they did before. In this way, I have improved day by day and week by week.

Now, with all this information, you have the tools to logically heal yourself. Inner healing is nothing more than a process of listening to your inner voices and then consciously and rationally figuring out what kind of reality those voices are going to create. If you don't like that reality, change the beliefs that are going to create it.

You can unveil negative behavior patterns by doing a stream of consciousness dialogue about why you can't have the reality you desire. This will bring all of your negative beliefs to the surface. Once examined, they can be changed.

This dialogue is most effective if you write it out. First, decide on the negative behavior pattern you want to change. Then, write the words, "I will never be _____ because..." As you write your paragraph with one sentence to a line, you will discover the beliefs that prevent you from creating what you want. In the margin, write down which inner characters are saying these things; this will tell you who is controlling your reality. Once you've figured that out, you can then write down the emotion that each character generates. You will discover that one of the root emotions crops up more often than the rest.

As I did this work, I became aware that my root emotion was shame and that it was spoken most often by my victim. The two other emotions that came up most often were fear and loneliness, which kept me paralyzed. My victim was self-hating and in denial of all her strengths. Because she was afraid of failure, she was not motivated to try. Because she was terrified of the humiliation that failure would bring, her desire to remain invisible was always uppermost in her mind. The desire to remain invisible caused me to create a reality in which I had few friends and absolutely no impact on anyone or anything around me. For someone who came into life to be a teacher and a healer, my self-hating victim generated a reality that made it impossible for me to reach my goal.

Once you unveil the inner characters that are generating your "fate," you too can begin the healing process. After you've written your paragraph filled with negative limiting beliefs, re-write it and change each belief to a positive affirmation. Then, with a well-defined intent, go after what you want with your whole heart. Even if you don't know how, know that help will be given to you as you journey on your way. Your Beloved is not just a figment of your imagination. They are your guide who can help you create the reality you desire. When you proclaim to the universe that you are ready, willing, and able to heal by changing your attitude, your entire resonance will change and you will magnetize to yourself a whole different reality.

There are also several things that you can do meditatively to convince your subconscious mind that you do want to change. The first thing you must do after you've unveiled negative attitudes that lead to defeat and failure is to decide absolutely and unequivocally that you don't want to be that way any more. Then, go into meditation and creatively personify your negative behavior pattern in form and say no to it, as I described how to do in the chapter on symbolic imagery.

Afterward, you can work with your Beloved in meditation. Tell them why this negative behavior pattern is hurting you and others around you. Feel your anger and resentment rising. Tell your Beloved that you are tired of the way you have been behaving and that you are now determined to change. Tell them how much you hate the behavior and how stupid you feel for doing it, if this is indeed how you are feeling. Tell them everything. This is the way you own the behavior as yours. Once owned, you can then do something about it.

Then ask your Beloved if they will help you to release the behavior and see what they say. They might give you advice. They might do a cleansing or healing ritual with you. They might surround you with light. They might reach into your body and pull out the seed or root of the problem. They might bring in angels. They might suggest you need to do more writing and thinking about it or do a creative project that symbolically releases it. They may suggest ways to further re-educate your inner voices or to refocus your attention on the positive. This kind of trance work is so much fun because you never know exactly what is going to happen until it does.

After you have performed one or more healing rituals with your Beloved, you will need to do forgiveness work. Perhaps you need to forgive yourself for being such a fool, too gullible or unaware, or whatever your particular limitations may be. Forgive those who unintentionally taught you those limited beliefs and don't forget to say you're sorry, at least in meditation, to all those you may have hurt with your negative beliefs. This can all be done in trance with your Beloved.

If you don't think you deserve to be forgiven, let your Beloved tell you why you do. When you punish yourself for your mistakes, you bury them deeper and go further into denial. Everyone deserves to be forgiven. Because consciousness is a continuously growing and evolving thing, we all make mistakes. No one can be held accountable for their ignorance no matter how devastating their behavior. In order to heal, you must forgive both yourself and others for the mistakes that have been made. As you work with your Beloved on these issues, your Beloved can be your guide to forgiveness.

After you've done the forgiveness work, you need to begin exploring what it will be like when you own your new positive beliefs. To own something means that you live it, teach it through your example, and *be* it. After you've done the challenging and sometimes painful work of unveiling negative beliefs, it's time to do the joyous work. Really think about what it's going to be like when you are free of the problem, the limitation, or the pain. Visualize it and feel it. Talk to your Beloved about it. Let them celebrate with you and add to your enthusiasm. Become playful and joyous in your meditations. As your relationship with your Beloved becomes more and more real to you, this kind of celebrating can have great emotional impact. Nothing is too good to be true. When you can let yourself be successful in your mind, you are much more likely to receive it physically.

After you've done the meditative work, you can then write affirmations or do art work and rituals around your new belief system. This will help you keep your thoughts focused on the positive, which is what will allow you to eventually receive it. That's all there is to it.

Raising your awareness into higher consciousness is the name of the game, and when you raise it to include more and more of the truth, there is no end to all the magic and miracles you will receive.

When you heal your negative beliefs by listening to the stories you tell yourself, you heal your attitude. When you heal your attitude, you can take charge of your life so that you can become all that you can be.

117

Everyone has a divine potential to fulfill, but by listening to inner characters who voice negative beliefs, that potential will stay hidden. Because the power of decision is your own, this need not be a lifelong pattern, for it is never too late to change. Changing, however, is dependent on your motivation. Decide for fear and it will be given to you. Decide for Love and it will be given to you as well.

The following chart summarizes the negative and positive characteristics of the inner voices.

	Negative	Positive
Judge:	perfectionistic	keeps you true to your goals
	critical	
	punitive	discriminating
	often says "should"	discerning
	social dogma	powerful motivator
	self-righteous	prioritizes activities
	rigid in their judgments	practical
		keeps you on task
Priest:	"true believer"	always searches for the light
	moral condemnation	
	self-sacrifice	curious about the esoteric
	deprivation	
	exoneration on the judgment day	unquenchable thirst and desire to know
	denial of contracting emotions	longs to be spiritual
		strongly committed

Cynic:	apathetic	skeptic who is highly protective of you
	searches for flaws	
	close-minded	examines facts closely
	paranoid	grapples with the unknown
	negative	
		gathers facts, does research

Mr./Ms. Together:	constant denial	calm, cool, collected
	superficial	practical
	keeps up appearances	grounded
	performs life	self-confident

King or Queen:	tyrant	born leader
	arrogantly superior	good organizer
	controlling	assertive
	dictatorial	positively authoritative
	misuse of power	sense of presence and deservingness
	pompous	
	condescending	appreciates luxury
		generous, wise, and giving

Inner Child:	self-centered	innocent
	insecure	divine
	needy	playful and full of laughter
	dependent	
	has abandonment fears	non-judgmental

	vulnerable	non-condemning
	self-indulgent	earthy, wild, and free
	irresponsible	
	"whines"	
	frightened of inconsequential things	
Inner Adolescent:	self-important	curious
	many "absolutes"	open to exploration
	inflate their ego by aggrandizing their bodies	endlessly creative
		delight in the new and unexpected
	either arrogant or self deprecating	
Rebel:	rebellious	positive outrage
	hard-headed	innovative
	stubborn	pioneering
	reckless	crusader
	self-destructive	
Adventurer:	rolling stone	curious seeker of the unknown
	wanderer	
	little perseverance	strong, energetic, capable
	rootless	
		learns from new experiences

Warrior:	destroyer	logical, rational
	violent	gets the job done
	ruthless	strong in commitment
	competitive	self-control
	wins at all costs	strategist
	end justifies the means	indomitable will to succeed

Romantic:	overly emotional	passionate
	clingy	devoted
	possessive	intimate and loving
	jealous	filled with desire
	overly dramatic	sense of esthetics
	unreasonable	innate ability to give and receive
	illogical	

Rescuer:	smothers you in love	can rescue your inner child and adolescent
	self-sacrifice is a form of control	
		creates faithfulness

Victim:	weak	can ask for help from their Beloved and surrender to the divine
	helpless	
	dependent	
	frequently sick	
	constant blame	
	self-pity	
	long-suffering	
	lonely	

depressed

desperate

hopeless

never takes responsibility
for reality creation

Bully: persecutor   a protector who says
no to overwork,
seeks revenge   worry, and stress

abusive

both passive-aggressive
and aggressive

vengeful

Martyr: combination of rescuer,   once healed, understands
victim, and bully   how to take complete
responsibility for
inconsistent   reality creation

filled with self-
righteous blame

filled with grievances

feels they are always
innocent and beyond
blame

Voice of fear root emotions: Voice of love root emotions:
shame, loneliness, fear,   happiness, peace, joy,
anger, hopelessness,   love, gratitude, trust,
despair, hurt.   optimism, hope.

Part Three

Cleansing the Energy Field

Chapter 8

Releasing Contracting Emotions

All emotions have a negative and positive polarity. In their negative polarity, they are contracting. In their positive polarity, they become expansive. When emotions contract, they create limitation and pain, causing one to become less of who they are. When emotions expand, they make us feel good. By freeing us from our limitations, they motivate us to become more of who we are.

It may be hard to believe that emotions like happiness and love, which are usually expansive and positive, have a negative polarity, but they do. Someone who pursues their own happiness irresponsibly at the expense of others is experiencing the dark side of happiness. Parents who smother their children in love, in the negative sense of that term, are creating a dark love.

Most often, however, the contracting emotions are the ones we have always thought of as dark, negative, and detrimental. Emotions such as hate, rage, envy, jealousy, greed, hostility, and resentment always cause contraction, which means that they create limitation and pain. It is not until one heeds the message their dark emotions are giving us that they begin to expand. Once they become expansive, they transform, becoming positive.

What are these detrimental emotions trying to tell us? They are nothing more than a wake-up call. As a wake-up call, they tell us when there is something out of alignment in our belief system. For example, if you are feeling jealous, you must ask yourself why. Do you believe that there is not enough (things, happiness, love, success, etc.) to go around? Do you believe that you are inferior and thus unworthy in some way? By examining the beliefs your dark emotions rest on, the feelings can actually point you in the direction of healing. This is when they shift from contraction to expansion.

Unfortunately, because the dark emotions are socially unacceptable, many people deny feeling them. The denial prevents ownership. Without ownership, one will never examine the beliefs they rest on. Without changing one's limiting beliefs, one's pain will be recreated over and over again. This not only keeps the dark emotions in place, it prevents behavioral change.

There are four specific ways pain manifests physically. The most obvious way is through disease which occurs in the physical body. The next is through accidents that happen to the body and thus result in pain. The third way is through conflicts. Conflicts always cause physical symptoms of stress, and they may also result in violence, leading to bodily harm. And the fourth way is through poverty. Poverty generally manifests as mental and emotional pain first, but it can eventually lead to physical discomfort, starvation, and even death.

According to our belief system, diseases, accidents, conflict, and poverty are a natural part of the human condition. Yet this is not necessarily so. They only seem natural to us because we have been taught limited beliefs that inevitably create etheric pain.

Etheric pain is the mental, emotional, and spiritual pain that results from beliefs that do not produce a productive, beneficial reality. In order to clear the energy field of etheric pain, two things are necessary. First, the contracting emotions must be expressed in a safe way. Secondly, the beliefs that create contraction must be transformed into positive productive ones. These positive productive beliefs will generate expansive emotions. An energy field free of etheric pain will both create and attract an altogether different reality than one that harbors it. Positive, productive beliefs will generate positive, productive behavior that heals everyone.

Non-productive beliefs lead to powerlessness. Not only do they prevent us from doing the things that lead to healing, they destroy the will. The will is our motivation. Someone whose will has been destroyed by their belief system is not motivated to heal. Although they may willingly purchase medical intervention or pray incessantly, they won't do the inner work necessary to heal the beliefs that create the inner pain. The reason people won't do this is not because there is something wrong with them. For the most part, we simply don't know what to do. We don't know how to transform limited beliefs into expansive ones. It is this ignorance that cripples the will and creates powerlessness.

Because of our ignorance of reality creation, our entire world is entrenched in a non-productive belief system. Disempowering beliefs create limitation. Limitation fosters envy, jealousy, rage, hopelessness, and helplessness, as well as every other contracting emotion there is. Limitation also fosters manipulation and control. Disempowered people whose lives are destined to disintegrate into disease, accidents, conflict, and/or poverty have no other recourse. Manipulation and control leads to domination, and domination creates greater pain. Through ignorance, we have created a circular belief system that imprisons us.

Once someone has found their will to heal because they've changed the beliefs that prevent them from doing so, they can stop denying their contracting emotions. Through ownership the emotions can be expressed and released. Because the contracting emotions must be expressed at the time they occur — which is usually before one's beliefs are examined — in this chapter I will discuss how to safely express the ones that are being generated by your present reality. In the next chapter I will discuss how to release contracting emotions that were generated in childhood and adolescence.

In the case of rage, the simplest way to release it is to express it immediately to the one who is triggering you. Unfortunately, many of us aren't in relationships that are authentic, so this is not always the wisest thing to do. Even if you are lucky enough to have an authentic marriage, in which emotional honesty is encouraged, your relationship with a boss, co-workers, relatives, neighbors, or teenage children may not be. Because we live in a world that is entrenched in a contracting belief system, everyone is going to have to deal with conflict and friction that either results from projection and/or denial at some time. Most of us will have to deal with these kinds of relationships many times throughout our lives. Knowing how to deal with these relationships constructively is of paramount importance if we are to gain the freedom that allows us to heal.

If it is not appropriate to express your rage directly to the one who's triggering you, as is the case with children, the mentally impaired, and the mentally irresponsible, you can diffuse it by doing etheric plane communication (otherwise known as EPC). However, because the source of the problem won't be resolved, the rage will only remain diffused until it is triggered once again. Why express rage if it won't go away? Because, by expressing it, you let yourself know just how much pain you have. Since suppressed emotion will eventually kill you by creating either disease, accidents, conflict, and/or poverty, expressing your rage is imperative if you are to remain healthy. But even more imperative than the expression of your rage is its resolution, which is what inner work is ultimately about. As you rise up above the belief system we are all entrenched in to see its logical consequences, you will eventually find your motivation to change it.

I define the etheric plane as anything that exists in the non-physical realm. Therefore, EPC has to do with communication with others who are not physically present. This communication can be done with people who are living now or who have died. EPC is also how one communicates with their Beloved, angels, guides, and other unseen friends who are non-physical, as well as with the inner child and adolescent. Since the communication occurs in the etheric realm, it is non-threatening. This gives you the freedom to be totally honest, saying everything that needs to be said. It also allows you to clarify the issues so that when you do express directly to your offender, you can do so with the wisdom that will allow the encounter to be positive.

In order to do EPC, you must first feel your feelings. If you are being overwhelmed by contracting emotions, verbally give yourself permission to have them. Tell yourself you have the right to have every one of your feelings no matter what they are. Also, remind yourself that it is imperative for you to feel and express them first before dealing with the evolved concepts of reality creation I have been describing in this book. Get out of your head and into your gut and prepare to "go to work." This is the way you set the mental stage for emotional release.

EPC is done by visualizing the offensive person in front of you and verbalizing your concerns and feeling. You can do this as a confrontation which occurs in your mind only, or you can get physically involved in the act by beating pillows or throwing darts at their picture or whatever it is that appeals to you. You can really scream and shout or you can just do it in your mind. Physical expression and release is not better than doing it meditatively. It all depends on your personality type and what makes you feel best in the end. For me, doing it all in my mind is more effective than doing it physically. If I do it physically, it usually turns into a performance and I don't get a lot out of it. For you, however, it may be just the ticket, so experiment and do what feels right.

When you do EPC it is important to keep expressing until you've felt not only the rage and pain but also whatever other emotions are underneath them. For example, you might tell the offender how much you hate them for what they did, how wrong they were, how outraged, humiliated, and ashamed they made you feel. You can tell them what an idiot they were for doing what they did and how stupid you feel for getting involved with them. Let your inner two-year-old kick and scream and throw a tantrum. Let your inner adolescent curse and use the worst language imaginable, if this is your style. This is the time to give yourself permission to express it all, no matter what it is. Therefore, do it with intensity and don't stop until you have said, felt, and done everything you need to say, feel, and do. Doing it with intensity and passion is the key. The more authentically intense and real you can be, especially in expressing your feelings and true desires, the more you will be healed.

If you want to add meditative visualization to the experience, go ahead and do so. Actually see yourself burning the offender at the stake or chopping them up into little pieces, if this appeals to you. Be creative! The only requirement is that you enjoy every minute of it. Let your suppressed hatred out and vent it in the etheric realm creatively, spontaneously, and intensely. When you do it in the etheric realm with your Beloved standing by to transform the energy as it is expressed, it does not hurt anyone and you will feel tremendous release afterwards.

Do not be surprised if, sometime during this EPC session, rage turns into deep pain. I have rarely done an EPC session that has not ended in tears. That is because underneath rage is usually humiliation and underneath humiliation is hurt. Once you begin to feel and express your hurt, you will have found the key to unlocking the pain in your body. Although it can be verbally intense, and perhaps even a visually violent and gruesome experience, EPC has great healing potential, as long as you are aware of your ultimate goal, which is to release contracting emotions and to transform the beliefs that created them.

If you allow yourself to get into a stream of consciousness mode, there is another amazing phenomenon that may occur while you are doing EPC. As you scream and yell your accusations, perhaps at someone who is a present offender, allowing one sentence to lead to another without censor, often times other triggering events and experiences from the past will come to mind.

As you allow yourself to keep free-associating, you may discover that although at first you started out yelling at your spouse or employer, you end up yelling at your father or mother or someone else in your early childhood. This will give you insight as to how you are projecting your feelings around the early offender onto the new one. As you keep expressing, you will begin to access the energy field of the child you were at the time of the original offense. Now you have gotten to the source of the problem where it can be healed. I suggest you then do a child rescue mission (explained in the following chapter) so that your inner child can begin to feel safe and loved. Once your child and adolescent both feel safe and loved and you, as their authentic inner parent, have re-educated and healed them, the "adult you" will no longer carry your child's projections into your grown-up experiences. In these cases, you will find that your rage at a present offender simply evaporates.

There are different ways of doing EPC other than verbally. It may be that you want to write hate letters that are never sent or tape record messages that you re-listen to over and over again until they stop triggering you. You can draw pictures expressing your feelings or choreograph dances. Be creative. Anything goes. The point is to keep expressing until you've gotten the feelings out of your system by discovering why and how you created the resonance that drew the conflict to you in the first place.

I have done an enormous amount of EPC with my ex-spouse as the target. Since we never resolved the conflict that led to the disintegration of our relationship, it has never been healed. Because we are tied together by our children, it is not a relationship I can simply walk away from. Therefore, it's a karmic relationship I have to deal with whether I want to or not. Because our post-marital relationship has been anything but peaceful, I have had to deal with my rage toward him over and over again. I have done this through EPC. In a way, he has been a good enemy for me. I have had to look at all the ways I have created my reality with him and why I chose him to be in my life. He has forced me to take responsibility for every comment I make. I have had to deal with every accusation he hurls at me and take a good long look inside myself to own the ones that were true. He has caused me to clarify my boundaries and to come to terms with my jealousy.

Many of these inner aspects of myself I discovered through EPC. It has been an invaluable tool for me to deal with emotions I otherwise would not have known what to do with. Although we create our reality either by directly causing it through our behavior or by allowing it to be drawn in through resonance, frequently we do not know how we are creating it. I had no idea how I was creating someone I considered to be so abusive to be in my life. I didn't recognize my own arrogance or take responsibility for the ways in which I triggered him. My ex has been my catalyst for figuring out how I create my reality through my behavior, my denials, my projections, my shadow, and my unconscious desire to attack.

Eventually, as I evolved my understanding of reality creation, I got beyond needing to do EPC with my ex simply because I began to understand the karmic lessons that had brought us together. As I chose to learn the lessons this situation had to teach me and then to heal the sorrow it had caused, he simply stopped triggering me. This is the way I was able to overcome many of the mental blockages my upbringing had given me. However, until these understandings occurred, EPC was the tool I used to help me blow off the steam of my rage.

EPC is also especially useful in expressing love. If someone's behavior is non-productive due to an immature belief system, giving them affection and approval may give them the wrong message. This can be devastatingly painful, especially if it's your teenage or adult child who is destroying their life through irresponsible behavior. Although you cannot change people who

133

aren't yet ready to change, you can give them your love just the same by doing it etherically.

Simply visualize the person you love in front of you and begin to tell them how much you really care and how your only desire for them is healing, change, evolution, and growth. Then visualize your loved one's higher self standing behind them. Ask their higher self for permission to penetrate the dark shield of negativity and pain that surrounds your loved one. With their higher self's permission, you can then etherically watch the love you are sending penetrate deep into their heart, mind, soul, and being.

Because we are spiritual beings who have a need to love, this kind of meditative work is especially healing, for the inability to give love can devastate the one whose gift is constantly refused. Love is more than just feeling and affection. It is also a set of actions that produce the feeling. As every parent who has a teenager bent on destruction knows, sometimes love must be tough. But through prayer and the kind of visualization work just described, the love and affection we all so long to give each other can be given. As you do it, you'll be healed. Since all minds are joined, your loved one will, on some level, receive. Eventually, in some lifetime, if not in this one, they too, will be healed. Your prayer work and visualization may become the catalyst that finally allows them to change.

EPC is also especially useful for doing forgiveness work. As you evolve along your spiritual path and begin taking responsibility for your behavior, you may begin to feel genuine remorse for things you have said or done in the past. As you do inner work, eventually you will have to deal with yourself as cause rather than as victim. All of us have been both victim and perpetrator at different times in our lives. Often, people who see themselves as victims take great joy in making others pay for what they've done. They do this in subtle and not-so-subtle ways, always claiming innocence.

Once you begin taking responsibility for reality creation and work toward evolving into your authentic self, you will inevitably discover that you were the cause of certain unpleasant events in your life. This will bring up many emotions, including remorse. When this comes up, you can express your remorse either literally, if this is appropriate, or meditatively, if literal apologies are either inappropriate or impossible.

For example, when I first began to do inner work and to see all things differently, I realized I had been a very jealous sibling and had made the life of my younger brother miserable. It wasn't until I became an authentic adult that I was willing to take responsibility for this. When I realized what I had done, I went to my brother and literally told him how sorry I was that I had behaved that way. Doing so made us much closer and I felt much better when I had cleared the air between us by recognizing myself as cause.

However, there were other people in my life I had also offended in some way. Most of them were people who had long since gone out of my life and I had no idea how to contact them. Therefore, I visualized them standing in front of me and said what I needed to say. As I listened for a response, most of them forgave me or gave me additional insights to think about.

You can also do EPC to finish unfinished business with someone, especially a parent, spouse, or child who has moved to an unknown location or who has died. Perhaps you never got to tell them that you loved them or that you forgave them before they left. It is never too late to communicate these things because you can always reach them through the etheric plane. Therefore, visualize them coming to you and say your final farewells, getting all that unfinished business off your chest so that you can finally let it go. Tell them of your love for them, your prayers for them, or make your apologies to them, asking for forgiveness. The point is to say what needs to be said so that you don't have to carry it around inside you any more.

I have also done a lot of EPC with my living children. Two years after my ex and I split up, they went to live with their dad. I felt incredible sorrow and grief about this. I dealt with that by doing EPC with them, telling them how much I loved them and how sorry I was for everything that had happened. This not only helped me to deal with my grief, it also helped me to deal with my feeling of failure. I believe that on some level they understood what I was communicating to them and that it helped them to deal with their own grief as well. When one does EPC, it is really the person's higher self they are communicating with. Though my children didn't consciously receive any message from me, their higher self did, and I was able to express my feelings to children who were otherwise too immature to understand.

I wish I could say to you that all it will take is only one EPC session to heal you when you are releasing emotions, but this is not so. It may take considerable time to figure out why you have created these various triggering situations. Also, when you are so angry at someone you want to kill them, it is usually because of a long history of triggering incidents. Because we have been suppressing rage since we were in the "terrible twos," releasing it is going to take time and conscious effort to achieve.

At this stage in our evolution, we have created a challenging spiritual situation for ourselves, one that may even feel impossible at times. We have embraced an insane belief system that imprisons us in limitation. Through resonance and dysfunctional behavior we are destined to create a reality of pain. It is inevitable that we will feel rage, hostility, and resentment as a result. Consequently, we must learn how to express these emotions appropriately because that is the only loving thing we can do for ourselves. In order to do that responsibly, we must become authentic human beings, and this will also take time and conscious effort to achieve.

To me, becoming authentic means that one feels all of their feelings all the time and never lies to themselves. It means they give their inner child and adolescent permission to speak, at least etherically, in whatever way appeals to them. It means that they own their projections and recognize their negative behavior patterns and choose to find a better way. It also means that they behave as a spiritual adult in every situation and come from their truth instead of inner lies.

It is impossible to create authenticity if one is suppressing their feelings. One can only get there by becoming whole, which means by recognizing and accepting all aspects of themselves, the light and the dark, the good and the evil, the male qualities of logical intellect and the female qualities of illogical emotions and then, maturely and responsibly, deciding to do what must be done to create healing, transformation, and change.

Most of us have been drowning in hurt all of our lives. When this hurt is released, it can feel overwhelming. I have cried an ocean of tears since I began doing my inner work. As I dived into the depths of my pain, it seemed like there was no end to my contracting emotions. I have spent days and days crying from the depths of my soul, sometimes not even knowing why. As the pain would let up and I would find equilibrium again, something else would trigger me and the tears would flow some more. I began to feel like I would never be healed and I regretted ever opening up this Pandora's box of pain that was overwhelming me.

If it had not been for my Beloved, I think I would have died of sorrow. That kind of pain is too terrible to face alone. It can only be healed when love waits at the end of it all. My Beloved has healed me because, without him to hold and encourage me, I would not have had the courage to keep on. When there is a wall of pain facing you, the only way to heal it is to go through, not around. Without angels, guides, and unseen friends to walk with you, how could anyone ever make it through the wall of their pain alone? Healing is a spiritual journey and, without the spirit to guide us, there is only more heartache at the end.

When I first began this work I was numb to the majority of my pain. The idea that pain is caused by lack of love was a new one to me. I lived a stressful life in which I was an overworked single parent of three young children. I quite literally didn't have time to feel my feelings. I did not have a Beloved or any spirituality at all to comfort me. I felt that if I could get myself from one day to the next without hurting too much, I could call my life a success. Since I didn't know the grandeur of Love, I didn't know what I was missing. I knew I didn't feel good about my life, but I didn't feel bad either. The truth was, I didn't feel much of anything at all. I went to work and did my job and, when I got my paycheck at the end of the month, I thought I was safe.

Many people have this attitude. Because their life is just good enough they think why rock the boat? Dredging up the past is anything but fun. People have their paychecks, their homes, their cars and boats and RVs. What more could anyone want? If inner work is so painful, why would anybody want to do it? It is because the pot of gold really does wait for you at the end of the rainbow. It has been called the Heart of Love, the Prince of Peace, and the Pearl of Great Price. It is the Light of Your Soul and the Glory of Eternity. It is you in all your splendor as Love created you to be. Isn't this a treasure worth finding? In my opinion, there is no treasure on earth greater than the real, authentic you. EPC is simply a tool that can help you to unravel your truth so that you can become the person you were always meant to be.

Chapter 9

Healing the Inner Child and Adolescent

You are not a body; you are a consciousness that radiates an energy field. Your energy field produces your body as a reflection of what is held within it. Your energy field is made up of invisible thoughts that generate emotion. Polluted thoughts produce toxic emotions. The body that reflects these polluted thoughts will fall prey to disease, conflict, and mental, emotional, and/or financial poverty, for these are the kinds of things that reflect a polluted energy field.

The energy field is like a stream. When you stand at the edge of a river, you do not assume that the entire river consists only of what is within your range of vision at the moment. You naturally assume that there are many miles of river you cannot see. It is also logical to assume that the particular expanse of river you can see has been impacted by all that has gone on before it. If someone upstream throws pollutants into it, it is certain that those pollutants will still be in the river when it flows into view. Even though the pollution may take a long time to accumulate to toxic levels, once it does, you will feel its impact.

This is precisely what has been happening to your energy field. If any of your past "selves" have polluted your "stream of consciousness" with limited beliefs, contracting emotions, or lack of love, you are going to feel the impact of this pollution as a body that is "unclean." Although it may have taken "time" for the pollution to reach its saturation level and become "visible" as disease, conflict, and poverty, you are still the sum total of all that has gone on before.

In order to heal, you must go back to the time and space when and where the pollution was put into the stream of your consciousness and heal it there. When you do, you can allow your past selves to express their true feelings. After that, you can heal their limited beliefs by teaching them the truth about who they are. Then, by showering them with the love and attention they deserve, you can create a situation in which the pollution is immediately dispelled. Once you have done this, the traumatic events of your past can be seen as experiences that add to your wisdom instead of ones that create pain. There is no other way that true, long-term, sustained healing can occur. That is because, once pollution gets into the river, there is no way to get it out other than to feel your feelings, re-write the script, and see your life differently.

This is why "talk therapy" does not usually work at a deep and profound level. Talking about the past does not re-access the energy field. Although it may help you clarify certain issues that allow you to understand why you have a dysfunctional behavior pattern at an intellectual level, it will not cause your past selves to release their toxic emotions or to have their disordered thoughts re-aligned and balanced. Talking about the past will not create inner safety. Neither will it heal you, for simply talking about the past will not create love.

Your past selves consist of your inner infant, child, adolescent, and young adult. I believe they also consist of hundreds of other incarnations, some of which may also need to be healed — but that is beyond the scope of this book. In order to purify the energy field, these aspects of the past must be addressed.

There are two different ways you can work with your inner child and adolescent. You will use the first technique for gathering general information. The second technique will be used when there are specific incidents that need to be healed.

In the first technique, decide before you go into trance on a general topic you want to discuss. Then, visualize your inner child or adolescent, noting details of face and form. Get a sense of their age, which will vary from meditation to meditation, as well as where they are located — their bedroom or favorite hiding place, etc. Then, using a stream of consciousness dialogue, let them start talking about the topic you've chosen. They may talk about several different events that were painful to them during the time period they represent, or they may only talk about one. As you do this stream of consciousness dialogue with them day after day for a given time period, you will gather a lot of information concerning the topic at hand.

For example, if you are trying to heal non-productive beliefs about your sexuality, go to your child in meditation every day for a week, and then the following week go to your adolescent, and simply ask them to talk to you about the events that have shaped their sexual identity. Ask them how they felt about these events. The more you can get them to feel, the better. Your child will say different things than your adolescent, for each will have their own unique memories to relate. Once they have discussed their feelings

142

with you, you can then focus on a specific incident and do a child rescue mission.

After discovering specific incidents that need to be healed, you must relive them in trance. This is the second technique for working with your child and inner adolescent. By reliving these specific incidents in trance, you can release the charge from your energy field. As you begin to work with remembered events, new memories will emerge from your subconscious mind. Eventually, event by event, as you continue your inner work, you will "remember" early physical, mental, and emotional experiences that were completely forgotten. This will only occur when you are mentally and emotionally prepared to handle such memories. If you are not, they will remain deeply buried in your subconscious mind and you will remain completely unaware of them.

Although shoving painful memories into your subconscious mind is a protective device that allows the child to survive traumatic events, if the memories aren't re-accessed and healed, the device that protected the child will kill the adult. Therefore, although you may not want to dredge up your childhood pain, it is imperative that you do so if you desire to cleanse your energy field of the toxic pain that creates disease. Once you have healed as many events as is necessary to cleanse your energy field, you can then move on to less painful meditative work. You will know when you are done when these incidents stop triggering you and you no longer feel the pain.

Re-accessing the energy field is a simple matter of visualizing the events leading up to the traumatic incident and then getting in touch with the feeling the events have caused. This is done by reliving the experience as if it were happening right now. The key in doing this is to realize that there is a difference between remembering the incident and reliving it. When you remember a traumatic event, you place an invisible wall of time and space between you and the experience. This keeps you from re-accessing the energy field of your former self and buffers you from re-feeling the feelings that the experience engendered.

To do this kind of inner work, you sit in meditation viewing the scene of the childhood trauma as exactly as you can remember it. You see the child and the other characters in the situation. You, the adult, watch what is happening as if you were watching it on a TV screen, through a window, or as if you are part of an audience at a theater. The adult becomes compassionate for the child in the same way you would feel compassion for a character in a play. The only difference is that this play includes something extra: Instead of just being a passive spectator, you, who have now become your child's or adolescent's authentic inner parent, protector, and advocate, get to step into the scene and help them rewrite it. You will not do this, however, until you have watched the entire incident from start to finish, or at least enough of the incident to arouse your compassion. At that point, after you have visually relived it by watching your child or adolescent re-experience the pain, fear, humiliation, embarrassment, disgrace, or whatever it was that caused them such pain, you can step in and rescue them. This is the part of the meditation that will completely depart from the actual memory. This is the time when you, as their adult future self, protect them from harm, re-educate and bond with them, creating an atmosphere of unconditional love.

Every childhood or adolescent memory you go back to in the second method should have essentially four separate components. First, you must relive the incident; second, all emotions must be re-felt and expressed, which also means those emotions must be evoked by the adult you if the child or adolescent seems to feel nothing. Third, the child or adolescent must be rescued, by either re-educating them or protecting them in whatever way is appropriate. And fourth, the child or adolescent must be healed. Healing always includes bonding, but it may also include a ritual of some kind. The more deeply in trance you are because you have made the meditation authentic and real by paying close attention to detail, the better you will be able to re-access the emotions.

The more you allow the child or adolescent to express, the greater will be the healing. Frequently, when I do this work, I stop seeing any pictures at all. I simply bring the child or adolescent up into my body and let them speak. By asking them questions I get them to dialogue about their experience. Therefore, even though no emotions may have been accessed in the beginning, eventually they will touch on a painful feeling and begin to express it. You will know if you are doing it right if your whole body is involved in feeling the feelings. If you make your visualization real, this won't be difficult to do.

Once the feelings are expressed, you, as the adult in their life, now take the role of their authentic inner parent. If you were parented incorrectly, you may not know how to do this. Becoming an authentic parent takes an enormous amount of wisdom. It means knowing how to love the child unconditionally and allow them to have all their feelings no matter how outrageous they may seem to you. It means letting them have their hatred and their jealousies, as well as their fears and frustrations. It means letting them be angry — screaming and shouting, hitting, or cursing. Being their authentic inner parent means that you not only let them have their feelings, you encourage them to have their feelings and even evoke them if they are in denial of feeling them. You will know if they are in denial by rationally examining a situation. If it should have been pain-producing but they feel nothing, or are feeling some other inappropriate emotion, you know that they are in denial of their true feelings.

For example, I once worked with a woman who had been date-raped by an older teenage boy when she was thirteen. Although what happened wasn't her fault, she had convinced herself that it was. The only thing her adult self felt was stupidity, born of shame. It took a great deal of convincing to get her to realize that hurt and rage were far more appropriate emotions. Once she, as the adult, understood how she had been oppressing her inner adolescent, she removed her self-imposed restraints. At that instant, her adolescent was allowed to feel her true feelings, express them, and heal.

After you have relived the triggering incident with your child or adolescent and encouraged them to express their feelings, the next step is to rescue them. This also takes an enormous amount of creativity on your part. It's my experience that the most effective rescues are the most realistic. However, you can be as creative as you want in this. The idea is to cause the child or adolescent to feel safe and loved. The purpose of the rescue is to teach them that someone in their life is on their side. Children frequently do not know when they are being abused, especially if the abuse is subtle. Therefore, you, as the adult, now become their protector and their advocate.

For example, if your child was abused by your parents, you will go back to a specific incident of abuse. After the experience is relived and the child removed from the situation, you, as the adult, will then go to the offending parent or parents and tell them, in no uncertain terms, to stop — and then tell them why. When you do this, you not only give the shame back to the people who caused it, you also clarify, in your own mind, why their behavior is inappropriate. This will not only heal your child, it will help you find your authenticity by assertively speaking your own mind.

In the beginning, your child and adolescent probably won't be capable of defending themselves. This is why you need to do it for them. However, there may be times that even you, as the adult, are still so petrified of an abuser that you cannot do this either. There is one person in your life who can, however, and that is your Beloved. They are not timid and shy and their love for you is enough motivation for them to go in and do whatever needs to be done to give the shame back to the person it belongs to. Although I do not always work with my Beloved when I am with my child and adolescent, he is always available when I call his name. It is certain that if I don't know what to do, he will. He has the ability to heal and rescue my inner child and adolescent in miraculous ways and I have complete confidence that he will always bring us to emotional completion, resulting in healing.

Eventually, your child or adolescent may be able to protect themselves. I have done an enormous amount of this work and when I first began doing it, both my child and adolescent were so hurt and shamed that they were incapable of any kind of self-defense or rational behavior that would keep them safe. However, to my great surprise, eventually they learned to defend themselves. At the point where they began aggressively defending themselves, I knew that my psyche had gone through some tremendous changes and that inner healing was genuinely taking place.

It may be that rescuing the child or adolescent does not include any kind of confrontation at all. Perhaps the situation in which they experienced shame, rejection, humiliation, or failure did not include abuse but was simply a result of the pressures of our culture and of not being adequately prepared to handle life's complexities. In this case, the rescue may only include loving the child and being there for them while they talk about and feel their feelings. Then you, as the wise adult, can help them prepare for life. When you do this, you give them the guidance they needed then but never received. You can talk to them about the complexities of life or the particular values of the culture you live in. In this way, you help them sort out the truth about any given situation so that it need not produce fear in them again.

Rescuing the child or adolescent also includes providing them with what is needed to feel physically safe and loved. If they need to be removed from a harmful situation like physical or sexual abuse, either remove them or educate them about ways to protect themselves. If it is a toy or pet they have always wanted that is the issue, give it to them. If they need to learn how to appropriately take care of themselves in a certain way, teach them. If they've been told to keep the abuse secret, tell the world. Do or say whatever the child and adolescent need in order to make them feel safe, loved, nurtured, and prepared for life. Never shame the child or adolescent or belittle them by making them feel their feelings and needs are unimportant. Even if an issue seems trivial to you, if your child or adolescent is feeling a lot of emotional charge around it, it is not trivial to them. Therefore, give them what they need to be rescued from their real or imagined pain.

Rescuing can take many forms. Often it is the child's own parents who are the offenders. Therefore, the child needs to be made safe from the very people they live with, people they may still love on some level. You, as the adult self, need to figure out what to do to make them safe without overstepping your boundaries. This is a more delicate situation than when the child hates their parents and would like to see them tortured and killed. In the latter situation, making the child safe may mean joyfully doing just that, but in the former situation, the rescue will call for greater creativity. When an abusive parent is still loved, you can visually separate out the "good" parent from the "bad" parent by watching them split in half. Then the child can acknowledge and love the "good" one and do what they would emotionally like to do to the "bad" one.

You must always do what the child wants you to do. Don't let your adult forgiveness get in the way. This is your child's meditation, and if doing something terrible to their abusers heals them and makes them feel safe, then do it. When your intent is to heal, what you do in meditation to make a child feel safe is not a means of attack. Once the rage and hatred is expressed, you will naturally move beyond it. However, if it is not expressed, you may be stuck in the unexpressed feelings for decades, so expressing it can only do you good.

Although all of your rescues will call upon your creativity, most of them will be less intense than torture and death. Perhaps all you will need to do to rescue your child is lock the abusers up. The key to the prison can then be given to your child or adolescent for safe-keeping. Another method is to give the offending parent to the angels or send the offender to a far-away planet for rehabilitation. You can bring in Rambo, Superman, or some other childhood hero or heroine to deal with your offenders if this appeals to your child's imagination. Do whatever you need to do to get the point across to them that they are safe from their offenders forever.

When I first began doing this work, I had an extremely difficult time expressing rage. I had no trouble with hurt or pain, but rage and anger were next to impossible for me to deal with. Therefore, I had to force myself to express rage and anger by learning how to bring them up. I did this in much the same way that I learned to express other emotions: I simply kept at it until my verbalizations finally touched a chord in me that sparked a volcano of feelings. Once that occurred, I could express the rage and hate I felt with gusto. Eventually, my rage almost always deepened into pain. Then, as my tears flowed, I could go to even deeper levels and express the feelings that were there.

If your child or adolescent wasn't physically abused, they probably won't be attracted to violence. Therefore, rescuing them will take a different form. Because I was not violently abused as a child, I rarely felt the need to be violent with my abusers in meditation. Usually, just having my adult self speak to them was enough, or removing my child from the immediate situation was all that was needed. However, my mind occasionally did very interesting unplanned things that allowed me to get the point across to my abusers that their abuse had consequences. For example, one time my child was hiding in a closet because she was going to be spanked. Much to my astonishment, when the closet door opened, I visually watched my child turn into a lion who devoured her abuser. Another time I watched my child turn into a dog who gnawed at my mother's leg for an abuse she had committed. These visualizations were totally unplanned. What the mind can come up with for healing is amazing if you do not censor it. In trance, anything goes, so let yourself have whatever comes.

After rescue work comes bonding and healing. Bonding is an experience of genuine, deep, unconditional love. When you are bonded to someone, you feel both physically and emotionally safe with them. You know that you can make mistakes in front of them and that they will neither laugh at you nor think less of you for what you did. As you bond with your Beloved, so must you bond with your inner child and adolescent. They must learn to trust you in the same way that you must learn to trust your Beloved. It does not always happen instantly. It may take time and many relived experiences before your inner child and adolescent will trust you enough to be authentic with you and before you will feel genuine love for them.

Many people have grown into adulthood hating the child or adolescent they were. They see them as clumsy failures who did stupid things. You need to realize that this is a product of shame, and that when your child or adolescent is free of it, you will no longer think of them as failures who constantly embarrassed you. The only way they can be healed is to surround them in love. Since nobody loved them unconditionally back then, you are their only hope now. Therefore, it is important to work toward bonding, even if you don't feel any intense emotion about it in the beginning.

You also need to give a voice to the part of you who hates the child or adolescent you were. Let it talk and say everything it needs to say. Bring all the self-hatred and negativity up to the surface and allow yourself to sit with these feelings for awhile. After you have done so, if you have external children of your own or if there is a child that you know and like, think about what it would be like for them if you had dumped all that hatred on them and what kind of adults they would grow up to be. Would they grow into happy, joyful, self-responsible people who loved life? Every time you tell yourself how stupid you are, you are actually telling this to your inner child. As you think of it this way, you can begin to realize why your adult self functions in the way it does.

You can also work with your Beloved on this. Tell them how you really feel about yourself and see what they say. They will not tell you to stop feeling the way you do, but they may be able to give you some things to think about to help you get over your self-hatred.

I did not have any difficulty bonding with my child, but I probably worked with my adolescent ten times before I bonded with her. Although I wasn't aware that I hated my adolescent, it seemed like I just didn't feel much of anything for her. My trance work with her seemed awkward, and I never knew quite what to say or do when I was around her. I'm not sure what it was that finally triggered me into bonding with her. It was as if, all of a sudden, I really understood that she was in pain and that she needed me. At that moment I felt the most incredible overwhelming love for her. I took her in my arms and we cried and cried together. After that experience, I never had trouble bonding with her again.

Because I felt greater shame as an adolescent than I did as a child, working with my adolescent has been one of the most important aspects of my healing. I was raised in such a way that I was totally unprepared for life. Since everything that I discovered about sexuality came from the media, puberty was a very unpleasant experience for me. I was one of those adolescents who went around with hunched shoulders and hair hanging in my face in the hope that I could make myself totally invisible. Even though I grew into a functional adult, the shame I felt about my body did not leave me until I began working with my inner adolescent. If I had not worked with her, I would not be writing this book, because I would not have had the courage to stand up and be visible by expressing my beliefs to you.

The last step in this trance work is to do a specific healing. Healing consists of doing a specific ritual to heal your child or adolescent of their etheric pain. During this time, I frequently work with my Beloved, angels, guides, and other unseen friends because healing work is their specialty. I often just hand the child or adolescent over to them. What happens next can be totally surprising to me. That is because they have insights and words of wisdom that I do not have and methods of healing that I know nothing about.

The healing ritual that will be used will vary according to the kind of problem being healed. If your child or adolescent has been sexually abused, you can be certain that they feel filthy inside. You can give them ritual baths, or the angels might want to hold them and touch them in such a way that they are cleansed from the inside out. I frequently work with the Goddess herself when it comes to healing my adolescent and preparing her to become a healthy sexual adult. The members of my inner sisterhood have loved her into healing, cleansing her, and grooming her as they teach her about the magic and wonder of being a woman.

My Beloved and I have worked with healing my inner child and adolescent in many other ways, as well. We have rubbed my child's etheric wounds with lotions and given her magic potions to drink that heal and soothe her. I have produced TV screens out of nowhere for my adolescent to watch so that she can see that eventually she does become a successful adult. My Beloved and I have taken my terrified child, who has just gotten old enough to read her first gruesome rape and murder story and who is screaming and crying that she will never be safe, to be baptized with healing water. Then my Beloved has placed the mark of Love upon her forehead so that she can never be harmed.

The rituals and healings that my inner child and adolescent have participated in have been rich and varied. They have been surrounded by complete, unconditional love. They have been tenderly embraced by angles. The Goddess has held them in her arms and rocked them. I, myself, have spent hours holding them in my arms and rocking them, soothing them with my words. My Beloved has taken them into the inner realms where I cannot see what he is doing and healed them there. He has played and frolicked with them as he has healed them of their inner pain. With my Beloved at my side and each of us holding my inner child's and inner adolescent's hand, my inner family is complete. In this way, my child and adolescent have healed, and so have I.

As you develop a relationship of trust and love with your child and adolescent, they will not be afraid to go back to painful incidents. They will actually look forward to working with you and they will always be glad when you come. Whether you believe this or not, they are still very real and very much alive inside of you. There is no such thing as time or space. That means that everything that ever was or will be is happening now. This includes all of your pain, which will stay unhealed until you take the responsibility to heal it. The truth is, your child and adolescent long to be healed just as you do. They long for a wise, loving adult to guide them. Also, they long to be nurtured by you. They need you as much as you need your Beloved, and in basically the same way.

Your energy field is not only intertwined with your Beloved's, who is a higher part of you, it is also intertwined with your child's and adolescent's. Perhaps one aspect of "becoming one" means uniting all these aspects of yourself into a single serene and peaceful bond of unconditional love. As you heal and evolve your child and adolescent, they will grow into the loving, healed adult you know you can be. As your Beloved heals and helps you evolve, you will eventually raise your vibration to the point that you blend and meld together with them. As you allow the Law of Resonance to lift the vibration of your inner child and adolescent, refusing to succumb to failure, your vibration must rise. Ultimately, this is how we are taken home. Doing your part by healing your inner child and adolescent is as essential as having your Beloved do their part by healing you.

This is an awesome process, and I cannot begin to tell you how important it is. Although you cannot change the memories that were, you can so totally change the meaning they had for you that they are not the same memories anymore. This is how you can eventually find the buried treasures from your past. By rescuing and healing the child and adolescent, you change their attitude about life. When their attitude is changed, the adult you will see all things differently, which is the true meaning of forgiveness. When your child and adolescent feel loved and cherished by you, they will feel safe and secure. It is their safety and security that allows you to explore your life in a creative, non-judgmental way. When they have learned to love life, so will you. Your love for life will eventually create a resonance that is bound to attract success.

Chapter 10

An Overview of Healing Techniques

I n this chapter, I am going to explain, in detail, how I healed
my lifelong allergies by using the techniques I have previously described. By examining how my healing progressed
and what I did to achieve it, you will have a better idea of how to
integrate this work into your life.

At the time I healed myself of my allergies, I had been reading
A Course in Miracles for two years. I was deeply involved in its
principles and philosophy. It was the basis of all the spiritual
knowledge I knew. I was also very much involved with a being
whom I simply called my guide, whom I had never visualized in
form or consciously communicated with. All of that changed when
I began taking a series of hypnotherapy courses, which taught me
how to do the visualization work I've shared with you in this book.

Hypnotherapy is a form of modern day shamanism. The two
are similar in that they both use conscious dreaming as a tool for
transforming one's reality. Once I discovered it, I fell madly in love

with the meditative process. I felt as if I'd come home. That is because being a conscious dreamer was a basic component of my spiritual heritage — a heritage that I believe was brought with me from many past lives spent doing conscious dreaming.

The way I was taught hypnotherapy was through both lecture and hands-on experience. In the morning we would be taught theory and in the afternoon the students would pair up and put each other into trance so that we could receive experience in doing it. In hypnotherapy, the trance state always has a goal. The facilitator would weave this goal into his words as he gently induced a client into a trance, and then the visualization would revolve around it. At the time of my healing, I was fairly inexperienced. I had perhaps ten hours of lecture behind me and still didn't really believe I could go into trance.

On the day my healing began, the lecture was about how to rescue the inner child. What I have told you in this book about how to run a child rescue mission was learned at that time. In the afternoon, I paired up with another student who was as inexperienced as I was. Neither of us really knew what we were doing and we were very nervous about the whole thing. After all, we had just been introduced to this material in the morning and hardly felt qualified to help each other run a child rescue mission in the afternoon. With our notes in front of us, we did the best we could.

When it was my turn to go into trance, my fellow student asked me what I wanted to work on. I told her about my lifelong allergies and that I wanted to find out why I had them. When she induced me into trance, she repeated this goal in the induction several times so that my unconscious mind would know the kind of material I wanted to receive. What followed was one of the most amazing trance experiences I have ever had.

After the induction, I found myself at the door of a house I had lived in before I was four years old. I don't know exactly how old I was in this visualization, but I could tell that I was very young because when my adult observer looked at my hands, they were very, very small. When you are in this kind of trance state, the mind seems to split in two. A part of the mind is still you, but the other part of the mind becomes the child of the past. Consequently, my adult self could see that my hands were small and could reason that I was young.

At this point, my facilitator told me to go into the house. I did so, but then had no idea what to do when I got in there. Finally, my facilitator asked me if there was a particular room I was attracted to. I said, "Yes," and walked into the kitchen. When I got there, I immediately burst into tears. My adult half had no idea why, but when my facilitator asked my child what was wrong, she immediately said, "I'm so hungry!" My facilitator then asked me if I could find something to eat. I looked all around. I looked in the cupboards and the refrigerator but I couldn't find anything to eat except for one baby bottle that had about an inch of milk in it.

Finally, my facilitator, who was feeling a little desperate, said, "Well, where's your mother?" Then I really became the child and, in a pouting voice, I said, "My mother doesn't feed me. She doesn't want me to eat." At that point, I really began to cry. What was occurring was a memory of how hungry I had been as a child. My mother was a very controlling woman who was neither nurturing nor loving. She would control me by not allowing me to eat. When I was hungry she would simply tell me that I had to wait for meal time, which might have been hours away. Since I was a very small and thin child, this seemed like an eternity to me. It was obvious that this kind of treatment had gone on since pre-verbal times, as represented by the small hands and the baby bottle.

The message I got from this early childhood experience of food deprivation was that I didn't deserve to be fed, nourished, nurtured, or loved. This realization triggered an intense emotional response in me and I began to cry as if my heart were broken. As my inexperienced facilitator frantically tried to remember what she had learned that morning in the lecture so that she could help me resolve this incident, she finally told my adult self to come in and love my child by feeding her. The interesting thing that occurred at this point was that my adult self could not find any food for her either. In frustration, my facilitator told my adult self to go to the market and buy something. Although I tried to do this, I could not visualize it. That was because my adult self had totally identified with my inner child's undeservingness. Because I had had such a restricted diet for so long, I could not even imagine feeding myself, much less my inner child.

After I came out of trance, I analyzed this point. I was struck with the fact that I had been totally unable to visualize feeding my inner child. As I thought about these things, I received a lot of insight into why I had my allergies. It was then that I realized I had to change my mental attitude about what it means to be nurtured, nourished, and loved if I was to be healed.

Before ending this trance session, my facilitator wanted me to bring my real mother into the meditation. My child was adamantly opposed to this. She was so hurt about not being fed that she didn't want to see her. However, my facilitator wanted me to bring her in, so I did. When my mother appeared, she didn't have any hands. Of course, in real life, my mother has two perfectly good hands. Therefore, seeing her this way was symbolic of her inability to nurture me. This realization had a massive impact on me emotionally and I began crying and sobbing as a lifetime of hurt came pouring out of me.

As the meditation continued, my facilitator asked me what my child needed to feel safe and loved. I simply said that I wanted to send my mother to God where she could be healed. Instantly I saw a bright light come out of the sky and flow into my mother's hands. It was a tremendously powerful and emotional experience to watch, and it was totally unexpected and unplanned.

This was one of the first directed meditative visualizations I ever did. I had no idea what I was doing and neither did my facilitator. We had been taught a few basic ideas about child rescue work that we had learned only hours earlier. That was all. Yet what resulted from that lecture was unforgettable. Because I released so much emotion and got in touch with so many unresolved issues, a tremendous amount of healing took place for me in that single meditation. Though I was not yet healed of my allergies, this meditation was an enormous first step.

That night, another amazing thing happened. While in bed asleep, the being I now call my Beloved came to me to do some healing work of his own. There were many times in the previous two years that my Beloved came to me in the middle of the night. He frequently did things to my energy field which I did not understand. I had gotten used to his visitations and always looked forward to them. If a month went by in which he did not come to do something magical to me, I felt deprived.

On this particular night he awakened me from a sound sleep. I got into the position I use for meditation, and he proceeded to take me back to a traumatic childhood event that occurred before the age of two. I was very deep in trance, only semi-conscious, and an odd thing happened physically: I released a tremendous amount of mucus down the back of my throat. All of my allergies gave me hay fever-like symptoms and I always had a runny nose, itchy eyes, and a cough. If I had been in normal consciousness or in light or middle trance, I probably would have choked. In the morning, I remembered my experience of releasing mucus, but I didn't remember the traumatic event that triggered it.

Was it at this point that I was healed of my allergies? No, it was not, because I still had other inner work that needed to be done to complete the task. For a while, I had been working with an inner guide I called the Divine Child. She was a little impish child that I had inside of myself who could do anything. I visualized her like the main character in Astrid Lindgrins' book *Pippi Longstocking*. She was always silly and full of laughter, which is not at all the way I usually am. She was not the wounded child I came to identify with later. Rather, she could fly and do all kinds of magical and wonderful things.

One of the ways I taught myself to visualize was to imagine doing silly and whimsical things with her. These were simple meditations whose only goal was to have fun and be creative. She more or less took over my healing at this point. I imagined she and I going to the market together. She would fly down the aisles with a shopping cart putting anything in there she wanted. We would have picnics together and I would visualize myself devouring foods that I hadn't been able to eat in years. I also introduced her to my wounded child and the two of them would play together and be silly. These were simple meditations but they had a tremendous healing effect because I was giving a message to my subconscious mind that it was okay to eat again.

I also did several other childhood rescue missions around food. Most of these I did without an external facilitator. Although it took a little practice, once I began doing meditative work and understood what the goal was, I had little problem doing it on my own. Most of the child rescue missions I ran came from incidents I remembered consciously. Others seemed to be purely imaginative. Obviously, the meditation I have just described that had so much impact on me could not have actually happened. There was probably no real event in which I found only a baby bottle with one inch of milk in it to drink and, of course, there was never a time when my mother didn't have any hands. However, it was the meaning and the impact this mediation had on me that made the difference in my healing. It was remembering how hungry I had been and how often my mother had deprived me of food that began the train of thoughts that led to it.

It wasn't until I did one final meditation that my allergies miraculously disappeared, almost overnight. In this meditation, I began to work with a being that my hypnotherapy teacher called my higher self. I really had no idea what that was. Therefore, when I visualized my higher self, I did not see it in form. I simply saw a rather vague light. I went on a journey to find this light and once I was deep enough in trance, I asked it why I had all these allergies. My higher self replied: "Food has never had power over you." I was surprised to receive this answer. I said, "It certainly seems like food has had power over me." My higher self then said: "Food only has power over you when you are not in your truth."

This simple statement had massive impact on me. When I came out of meditation, I really thought about it a lot. If food didn't have power over me, I should be able to eat anything. Because I was taught to believe that food was the problem, this didn't seem possible, for my allergic reaction to certain foods was immediate. So I began to listen to the stories I told myself. Before, when I approached eating foods I had been allergic to, my first thoughts were, "I'd better not eat this food. It will make me sick. I will pay for it for days. I am being ridiculous to even think about eating it." After I did my critical analysis of the problem, taking into account what my higher self said, my approach was entirely different. Now, when I approached eating food that I was allergic to, I simply said, "Food has never had power over me. It only has power over me when I'm not in my truth." This became my new mantra, and the stories I told myself about my own health and well being totally changed as a result of all the new insights I had received. In a relatively brief period of time, my lifelong allergies totally disappeared and I could eat anything. I consider this to be one of the biggest miracles of my life. To be able to eat anything I wanted after a life time of restriction made me into a meditative visualization believer for life.

To summarize, let's look closely at exactly what I did. First and foremost, I worked with rescuing and healing my inner child. I worked at reprogramming my subconscious mind to accept eating again as I visualized my Divine Child feeding me. I worked with my higher self who told me the truth. I changed the stories I told myself about my own health. I released many emotions and uncovered and transformed many limited beliefs that were not serving me. And, of course, I did have just a little miraculous help from my unseen friend I now call my Beloved. From start to finish, not counting my two years of devotion to *A Course in Miracles*, which had prepared me to receive this, my healing took about five weeks. Not bad for a novice, I'd say!

Chapter 11

Preliminary Steps

Since your Beloved will not come to you until you are ready to receive them, there are certain preliminary questions you can ask yourself before actually trying to meet them. Answering them will help you unveil negative behavior patterns that are obviously standing in your way. They will also give you clues to inner child work you can do. If these questions are answered honestly, your journey will accelerate, saving you an immeasurable amount of time. Honesty is the key word in all spiritual work. Since your Beloved is a part of you, they are instantly aware of any lack of authenticity on your part. If you aren't yet ready to receive them by being honest, they won't come to you, for they know you don't really want them to.

Therefore, the first question you can ask yourself is whether or not you truly want your Beloved in your life. A "yes" answer will mean you are ready to give over, to their guidance, every thought or belief you have ever held. You need to be willing to have the thoughts that are true strengthened, the thoughts that are untrue removed, and the thoughts that are only partially true purified. If you are not willing to do this, how can your Beloved heal you?

Because it is your beliefs that make you sick or well, this is essential. If you happen to believe you are not worthy of receiving divine Love, how can they teach you of your own worth unless you are willing to let that thought go? Once you are willing to accept your worthiness, your Beloved will have massive transformative impact on you. Are you ready for this kind of impact?

Are you really ready to change by purifying the beliefs that prevent it and strengthening the ones that achieve it? This kind of change entails enormous self-responsibility. When you are ready to be this responsible, your Beloved will move heaven and earth for you, as they help you to receive the insights that will allow positive change to unfold.

Once you are in contact with your Beloved, you will realize that there is nothing that you do alone. Already, you might have the sense that they have been reading this book with you, watching and waiting. They are watching you to see how receptive you are to these ideas. They are waiting for an honest invitation to become part of your life and be one with you.

If you decide that you're ready to experience this kind of oneness, you can ask yourself the next question, which is, "Why don't I believe I deserve love?" This may seem to be an odd question to ask yourself at this time, but it is my experience that most people don't feel they deserve love. I certainly didn't. In fact, all of my healing has been dependent on my changing this belief and expressing all of my painful and distorted feelings about it.

The reasons you may feel undeserving of love are legion, but you will probably find most of your reasons center around not feeling worthy. "I'm not good enough to be loved. I do bad things. I never do anything right. I'm a failure. I have no talent. I'm stupid. I'm not beautiful enough." And so on. These are just a few of the reasons you may find rumbling around in your mind. If you don't ferret out these beliefs and change them, they will keep you from undertaking this journey.

Although uncovering beliefs concerning undeservingness can be a very painful process, I encourage you to undergo it with as much emotion as possible so you can begin to feel the impact these beliefs are having on you. By letting subconscious beliefs come up without judgment, you can begin dealing with their effects. Judgment is a numbing device that will cause you to stop feeling and, thus, stop owning what these beliefs are doing to you. Therefore, go deeper into the feelings, no matter how uncomfortable they are. Allow yourself to feel your self-loathing if it comes up. Feel your sense of unworthiness if it's there. Let your ego rant and rave about how this journey is not for you, and that it can't possibly be true that someone such as your Beloved even exists, much less loves you unconditionally. If you feel, as I did, that you have never truly been loved, your feelings about this subject will be intensely painful.

In writing this list, you will become aware of what has been keeping you from healing. Since each of the items on your list will be emotionally charged, it may bring to the surface a great deal of pain you have been denying to yourself. These are just some of the beliefs your Beloved must take from you in order to heal you. When you have exhausted yourself on this list, both literally and figuratively, it's time to go on.

The next thing you can do is to write a paragraph about why love will heal you. We all need love. Everyone knows this. Even our lofty scientists have admitted it. But why? Why do infants who are not touched and nurtured die without love? It's not a physical need. It's an emotional need, and so pivotal to who we are as spiritual beings that we cannot survive without it. If we do survive, our personalities become warped and we will degenerate as human beings.

Some of the statements in your paragraph may be: "Love will heal me because it will bring me happiness. When I am happy I will feel good about myself. Once I feel good about myself I will be able to ... (make a list here). I will be in peace." And so on. These are the kinds of statements you will be looking for.

Once you write this paragraph you will know why you are choosing to undertake this journey and what the benefits will be to you when you know, in the depths of your heart, that you are truly loved by your Beloved. These will become the reasons that will keep you going, no matter how absurd the process seems to be. These reasons will become the goal that you focus your attention on. They will become the ends you seek and, as you participate in this journey, you will realize that your Beloved is the means. You will know why finding your Beloved is more important to you than owning a mansion or having a million dollars. In short, you will know why this journey is worth your total effort.

You can ask your Beloved to help you write this paragraph. Just ask, in the silence of your heart, why you need love. Either immediately, or sometime in the next day or two, answers will come to you. Perhaps one of the answers might simply be that you long for it and, until your longing is fulfilled, there is no room in your heart for anything else. Your Beloved will have much to say to you. Let them place thoughts in your mind and see what you can come up with.

Again, be honest with yourself and take your time. Allow your emotions to come up and allow yourself to feel the longing in an unrestricted way. The more you think about love and why you want it, the more you will long for it. The more you long for it, the more you will desire it. The more you desire it, the more you will create it. As you long for it, you will be sending out a psychic beam of light to your Beloved that will flash, like an arrow, straight into their heart. They will respond with an arrow flash of their own, so be prepared for miracles!

There is one more list to be compiled before we begin the actual work. In this list you are to write down all the reasons why you can't possibly succeed in receiving love and making the journey to your Beloved a success. These are all your ego's reasons why you can't have what you want. They will come up anyway, so you might as well face them head on. In this list, you will include such statements as, "I don't believe any of this. I'm not disciplined enough. I'm not smart enough to do this kind of work. I don't have time. This is ridiculous. It can never work. Fantasies are stupid." And so on.

In truth, it is this list that is the most limiting because in it lies your lack of motivation to change. It will contain all the reasons why your Beloved does not exist, so why try? If you cannot clearly see your way to an achievable goal that has significance to you, your motivation to continue in the face of all your doubts and fears will be lacking. For this reason, it is important to write this list so it can't subconsciously control you.

Even if you feel very enthusiastic about meeting your Beloved and feel you can make an honest commitment to do so, there will still be times when doubts will assail you. That is because there will be nothing within the ego's world of logic and reason that will encourage you to make this journey. The world does not believe in unseen beings who can have a positive, loving impact. Even if you, yourself, do not agree, the world's beliefs will still have massive impact on you simply because you will not find any support for what you are trying to achieve. Since the core of this journey is active imagination and visualization, others may actually try to discourage you in your pursuit of it.

Both the secular and religious world actively denounce fantasy. The secular world does so because it believes it is worthless. The religious world does so because it believes fantasy is the work of the devil. Beliefs related to either of these concepts will get in your way. If you don't want them to control you, you must bring them up and consciously decide if they are true. The fact is that fantasy has both a negative and positive polarity. It is my opinion that in its negative polarity it is, indeed, worthless and "evil." In its positive polarity, however, it is both valuable and healthy. In order to keep it in its positive polarity, one must be consciously aware of how to do that. If your moral intent in meditation is negative, your fantasies certainly won't have a beneficial impact.

After you have made your list, I suggest you rewrite it. This time, after each statement, you could add the words, "...but perhaps I am wrong. I'm willing to see things differently." This will give your Beloved just the invitation they need to step in and do their work. This is a beginning step in opening up your subconscious to question its deeply held beliefs and attitudes. It is a statement that says you are willing to change. It is also a statement that says you are willing to be taught the truth. You have now begun to question your tightly organized belief system, and your journey will progress much more quickly.

A statement that previously said, "All this stuff about the Beloved is nonsense," will now read, "All this stuff about the Beloved is nonsense, but perhaps I am wrong. I'm willing to see things differently." You can see how the energy around this

169

statement has completely changed. You've admitted your doubt and given it a voice. By saying you might be wrong, you've opened yourself up to doubt the doubt. By saying you are willing to see things differently, you have paved the way for Truth to enter. This is all that is required of you because your Beloved will do all the rest. Eventually, the Truth will enter of its own accord until the time comes when you never doubt again.

At this time, it would be advantageous for you to begin saying affirmations about meeting your Beloved. They might go something like this: "My Beloved is with me now. They watch over me, protect me, and keep me safe. They want to be with me as much as I want to be with them. My Beloved touches me with their words and heals me with their love," and so on.

You might also address them in the first person. They are already with you, whether you know it or not, and are already listening to your thoughts. Therefore, you might say, "I love you and I want you. Come to me. I need you so much. I want to feel your love within me now." Place all of your feelings into this communication. Your Beloved is really listening more to your feelings anyway. Thoughts and beliefs can and do lie, but your feelings cannot. If you cry out to your Beloved from the depths of your soul, they will respond to your authenticity and you will be answered.

Once you have completed all the inner preparatory work I have suggested, you will be ready to begin the journey to your Beloved. The more honest and consistent you are, the more prepared you will be for what is to come. Also, the more time you are willing to spend on your healing, the better will be your chances for success.

Remember, because of the false teachings of our society, you may have spent your whole life programming your mind to fail at love. If that is the case, you have told yourself thousands of negative affirmations every day about your lack of self-worth and your inability to receive love. Though your healing will take but an instant, it will take you time and consistent effort to remove all the blocks you have to the awareness of Love's presence, which is already within you, so that you can embrace it in your life.

From the day you begin this journey, new insights about Love will continuously be revealed to you. You will truly begin the journey the day you realize you are inadequate to be your own teacher and sincerely ask, with your whole heart, to be taught how to experience love. At that moment the door will be opened to you. Whether you know it or not, your Beloved will enter and your healing will begin.

Chapter 12

The Journey Home

Shall I go to the waterfall — the one with the high, rocky walls, the dappled green ferns, the sunlight streaming through in sheets of light like bars of gold? No, not there. How about beside the lake, up on my smooth cool rock? Shall I watch the water, as slick as glass, that mirrors the rainbow colors of heaven above? No, not there either. Shall I stand by that giant fir tree over there in the meadow, the one with the gnarly branches and the bird's nest way up toward the top? Shall it be here that I wait for my Beloved to come and be with me?

Suddenly, a scene unlike the rest flashes through my mind — a starry night, a black dome with pinpoints of light sprinkled across the sky.... It is the cosmos I see.... I am standing in the very center of the galaxy. Yes, this is how I shall enter in through the door of everything, and, in my spirit body, begin to commune with my Beloved.

As I stand beside the still waters of my safe place, staring up into the beauty of the night sky, I hear a quiet footstep, the snap of twigs, a rustle of grass. The next thing I know my Beloved's hand is upon my shoulder. In an instant I am in his arms, cuddled up against his chest. His energy encircles me as he holds me close. I look deep into his eyes and he looks deep into mine. "I love you," I tell him for the ten-thousandth time. "I love you so."

We begin to talk about this and that, the book I'm writing, some new insight I received today. He holds me tight but tenderly as we play and laugh and tease. The night's darkness wraps itself around us. We are alone in all the world, my Beloved and I. A sigh of deep contentment escapes my lips. Standing under a night sky of brilliant light, he begins to touch me lovingly. I desire him so. "Will you blend with me tonight?" I ask. The answer is always yes.

We begin a ritual I have experienced many times, of blending our energies together. In and out of form we go. Abstract energy, to form, to energy again. I see us in my mind's eye blend and mingle as colored light, a myriad of glimmers of sparkling love, becoming one.

I now feel him in my body and all around me. I bring him all the way in with a deep breath. The breath of fire begins to fill me up and expand, turning every cell in my body to glowing light. I become filled with the most glorious sensations. I breathe him in again and fill my body to overflowing with the illumination of his love.

As he touches me mentally, emotionally, physically, and spiritually, he tells me he longs for me to come home to be with him again. My whole being yields to our desire. "I love you with my whole heart, my whole mind, my whole being, and all my soul," I say to him. He tells me he desires to consume me with his love, to devour me with his light. He asks, "Will you surrender all your darkness to me? I will take it and meld it into a glowing coal of total ecstasy." I hold my breath. I am so filled with his love I can barely breathe. "Yes," I finally manage to say.

As he longs for me, I long for him until our two Selves meet in a wonderful explosion of the most intense pleasure I have ever known. He is the light and I am the dark and in our oneness, all is whole.

I feel nurtured and cherished as I lie, spent, within his arms. He holds me so tenderly. We may talk some more or I may drift into sleep with his arms around me protectively. I know that he is within me and I am within him, and together our two hearts beat in a symphony of love and harmony that is without end in its ability to heal and give. I know that within our union, all is complete and I am satisfied, knowing that it is our shared love that has made it so.

There is nothing in all the universe that could be more desirable to me than this. Our intimacy has fulfilled us both. Joy, pleasure, and love have become the center of our being. I rest secure within his arms, knowing that there is a universe of loving thought held forever safe within the heart of me. As I experience the meeting of heaven and earth and learn how to raise my vibration to match my Beloved's, he teaches me to love life again. He teaches me that there is nothing I cannot do if I truly desire it and that nothing is impossible as long as he and I are one. He also tells me that there is enough love in our two hearts, beating in synergy, to heal the entire world.

It is this love that is our gift to you. As you take the torch we light, you will begin a journey of discovery. Into the void you will go to bob and float on a rainbow sea. The earth will be your ship, the winds your sail, your spirit the fire that will light your way. Though the winds of time will blow you through stormy seas and sun-drenched days of lifetimes without number, each lifetime will be but a new horizon filled with experiences leading you forward on an evolution in consciousness that ends with Love. When you have done all you came to the physical plane to do and learned all you can from being in a body, your journeying will have but one goal: beyond time and space and without fear, you will face and heal the shadow self that brought you here. As you make the decision to walk through your own personal darkness, you will ignite the light that seeks your soul. Then, when your two sparks become as one, you'll go home, the journey done.

During this voyage, you will learn who you are. You will explore all the dimensions of your being in the many worlds and on all the planes of your reality. But first, your Beloved will walk with you on a journey through the mists of the physical plane. They will teach you how to heal your past so that you can create a brilliant future of love with them. You will discover that, in your essence, you are nothing more and nothing less than a divine child of light who has come to the physical plane for a single purpose — to learn how to love so that you can create, on earth, heaven above.

With your Beloved by your side, the two of you will journey forward together. Into the depths you will travel, leaving behind you a trail of light. As your Beloved enters into you and you enter into them, they will use your hands and feet, your eyes and ears. They need your voice to speak the words of wisdom that will heal the world of all its pain. They need you to make your unique map of love and light so that others can follow the trail you made.

Come journey with us, my friends. Without arrogance, we will hold each other's hands. In trust and safety we will go, wiping away each other's tears, healing and cleansing, singing and praising, as we walk along the path to Them. Our Beloveds will teach us how to awaken gently and touch us with their loving words. They are not fooled by our past failures. Our errors of thought mean nothing to them. They know that love can heal all that is, and as they help us to our feet, we will learn to dance the dance of eternal life with them.

Within the synthesis of all creation, there is always a safe passage for those who seek the light. With your Beloved's hand in yours, you will journey straight into the light of love, where your heart's desire is available for all to see. As you begin to understand that the mending of your heart has always been your final goal, the end you seek, your destination and your one desire, you will gladly sail the seas of life with them.

The cost of love is not too great. All that is asked is that you allow your Beloved to unlock the chains that will set you free. On wings of light, they will carry you over all the pitfalls, past all the pain. The journey is not long. It ends where it begins, in your heart of hearts, where a dual spark burns as a single flame.

Part Four

The Meditations

The Induction

In this section of the book are several printed meditations that will allow you to begin creating your relationship with your Beloved. As I stated in the chapter called Meditative Visualization, you can use them loosely from memory as a script or tape record them yourself. Once you read the first three parts, you will be ready to begin doing the meditations described here.

I suggest you do them slowly. Allow yourself to work with what you have learned from each meditation for a while before you go on to the next. If you do a lot of fantasy work around each meditation, it will be fun and informative, and each time your meditative skills will increase. I also suggest that you do the meditations in this book in the order they are given, because they are designed to take you on a specific journey of self discovery. Although they begin simply, they become increasingly more complex as you gain skill and understanding.

In the first meditation, all you will experience is your safe place

— but in a very unique way. In the second and third meditation, you will begin to experience your Beloved. After you have done that, it is very important to spend time fantasizing about your Beloved, talking to them and pretending to be together. The safe place and your Beloved are an integral part of all the rest of the meditative work in this book. After you have spent some quality time with your Beloved, you will be ready for the rest of the meditations.

You will have set the stage for some very intriguing and healing work to begin. All your meditative visualizations will be done in a light or middle state of trance. There will never be a time when you will feel out of control and, if you are listening to a tape, you will always be completely conscious of what is being said by the facilitator. If you do not like what is happening in a meditation, simply end it by opening your eyes. If you should want to re-enter the trance state, close your eyes again and begin to visualize.

Before each meditation is an introduction. It will briefly describe the focus of each meditation, as well as give you specific instruction on how to make your meditative work more vivid and real so that you can gain deeper insights.

Before doing a meditative visualization, it is good to do an induction that will help you relax your body and deepen your trance. An induction is merely a set of verbal cues you give your body to let it know it is time to go into trance. Your body has memory, and as you induce yourself into trance over and over again, your body's cells will learn to remember it. After a while, the cells in your body will react to the induction on cue with little mental effort on your part. If you give yourself the same induction, and do it in more or less the same body position each time, it won't be long before going into trance will become effortless.

There are many methods of self-induction, and only you can determine which ones work best for you. Many people focus on relaxing their body, part by part, and then count themselves down into trance, deeper and deeper, using numbers as a cue. Other people visualize themselves floating through the clouds or wandering lazily on the beach or through a forest. Still others blank their minds, seeing and feeling nothing, using no words at all. Some will do the opposite and say affirmations or mantras until their body is relaxed. Other people will use special breathing techniques or body postures.

The object is to relax your body and let go of the outer world. Both of these objectives can be accomplished simultaneously when you consciously focus on relaxing your body because, by doing so, you must focus your attention within.

I am going to give you a simple induction to start with. If you choose to use it, you can either tape record it or mentally tell it to yourself with your own inner voice. Sometimes I prefer one method and sometimes the other. In the beginning, I found I could relax more deeply if my voice was on tape. That way I didn't have to worry about remembering what to tell myself. I also had to keep up with the words on the tape, however, even though they might not have matched my inner pictures — so using your own inner voice has advantages, too.

The induction I am about to give you is a simple one. If you decide to record it, your voice should carry a soft and gentle cadence and rhythm. It is very different in character and quality than the voice you will use when taping the meditations themselves. That is because the induction has a different purpose than the meditation. The purpose of the induction is to put you into a relaxed state of mind. The purpose of the visualization, however, is to create interest so that your conscious mind becomes completely absorbed in its inner pictures. Consequently, the meditations should be taped with a very expressive and alive voice.

This difference is significant because if you tape the meditation without expression, in the same way that you tape the induction, you will end up falling asleep and the meditation won't evoke any emotions. Since this is exactly the opposite of what you are trying to achieve, it is important to understand how to prevent this from happening.

When you tape the induction, imagine that you are a mother cradling a child who needs comforting. Make your voice soothing and speak slowly. Follow the rhythm of your breath, in and out. You are trying to slow down and relax all your body functions. This will happen naturally if you speak at a slow and even rhythm, saying only a few words for each breath. There will even be times when you may want to break a word into its syllables, saying just one syllable for each breath. An example would be the word "relaxation," which can be broken into four breaths: re ... lax ... a ... tion. This will give you an idea of how slowly and rhythmically you should speak. Remember, however, that there must be a balance struck between relaxation and attention, because if you relax too deeply you will fall asleep. This problem can be solved by focusing on your voice as it speaks to you and placing your attention on what it directs you to do.

The Induction

Now to begin the journey to meet your Beloved: Take a deep breath and begin to feel your body relax ... relax and go deep ... deep ... deep into a gentle relaxation, a gentle state of perfect peace. As you do your last little wiggles and scootches, perhaps you can let go of all the cares and the tensions of the day. Perhaps also, you can notice any sounds around you, the ticking of a clock, traffic noises, children playing in the next room. As you notice these sounds, perhaps they can take you deeper into trance, deeper into relaxation.

Now, focusing on the sound of your voice as everything begins to slow down (if you've taped this), remember a time in the past when you went into a deep place of perfect peace, a deep place of total trance. Now allow these memories to resurface in every cell of your body so that your body can simply take you there, into total peace, total trance, letting go, letting yourself go deep, breathing deeply, down, down into to ... tal ... re ... lax ... a ... tion.

Perhaps now you can feel your toes relaxing, now your feet ... ankles ... calves ... knees. (Focus your attention on each body part to give your body enough time to respond, spending longer on those parts of your body that hold tension.)

Now your thighs are relaxing ... your pelvis ... your buttocks. Now you can feel your back relaxing, lower back ... middle back ... and upper back. Now your front is relaxing ... abdomen ... stomach ... and chest. Now your arms and hands are relaxing ... your neck and shoulders. Perhaps now you can feel the relaxation flowing into the muscles of your head ... the back of your head ... sides of your head ... and crown of your head. Now the relaxation spills over into your forehead ... temples ... cheeks ... jaw. Now your eye sockets are relaxing ... your eyeballs ... your eyelids.

Now mentally peruse your body and notice any body parts that still need relaxing. Gently say to that body part in your own inner voice, "Relax, relax and go deep, deep into peace, deep into relaxation, deep into trance." Do that now ... (pause for a few moments here).

In order to take you into an even deeper state of relaxation, I will count from five to one, and when I get to one, you will be at your safe place at just the right time of day.

Five ... going deep into relaxation, deep into trance, knowing that your Beloved awaits your call.

Four ... letting go of all judgments and expectations of the way you think this meditation should go. Letting go of all your thoughts and feelings. Letting go of all need to control.

Three ... letting go, going deep, knowing that whatever is supposed to happen will happen, and that you are in the hands of spirit.

Two, one.

(End.)

That's all there is to it. You will find this to be a very effective induction. It is simple, involving conscious attention to your body. It reminds your body that it has its own memory and gives your body permission to use its cellular memory to relax you. If there is noise or distraction, it instructs the unconscious mind to use it to take you deeper. The relaxation is deepened by counting down, giving yourself numerical cues to do so. You can go slower or faster, depending on how long it takes you to consciously relax your body as you place your attention on each body part.

By going to your safe place, you set the stage for certain sensory stimuli to activate specific chemical responses in your brain to put you into a very deep state of trance. Although this induction is simple, it gets the job done quite efficiently and should take no more than five minutes to do.

It is also a good idea to bring yourself out of trance the same way every time. The purpose of this is to tell your body that relaxation time is over and it is now time to become grounded again on the physical plane.

When I bring myself or anyone else out of trance I always use a simple formula. I say, "Coming out of trance now, counting from one to five. One ... beginning to feel myself come back into my body. Two ... coming all the way back. Three ... wiggling fingers and toes. Four, opening my eyes, and five. Welcome back, awake, alert, alive and refreshed." When I say this, my voice rises and becomes stronger with each number I count so that when I get to five, I am fully awake and alert.

Meditation 1

Discovering the Safe Place

The first meditation you will be taught to do is to find your safe place. I would suggest that you review the chapter on meditative visualization before you do it. Your safe place is just that — a place where you feel safe and where nothing can harm you. It needs to be out of doors where there is a great deal of sensory stimuli. That is its only parameter. Once you find your safe place, it will not change, although you will notice more and more details about it with each passing meditation. The immovable objects there — the rocks, trees, water, worn passageways, land formations — will always be permanent. However, there is much about your safe place that will change with each meditation.

Although I will tell you to go to your safe place at just the right time of day, the right time in one meditation might be in the morning, another in the evening, and so forth. It all depends on your particular mood and the needs of this particular meditation, and will therefore vary from meditation to meditation.

Besides the time of day, there are other details in your safe place that will fluctuate as well. These are the things in nature that always change: the weather and the seasons. In some meditations, you might also find animals, birds, or insects. In others, there might be fairies and elves. The act of looking for these details will always take you deeper into trance. Therefore, it is important to go to your safe place with an open mind and see what appears without having preconceived ideas about what you will find there. If you want your safe place to be real to you, it needs to be filled with variety so that it reflects this reality. The more imaginative and creative you can be, the more real your safe place will become.

After the induction, you will begin to see your safe place detail by detail. Take your time to do this and go slowly. At first, your imagery may change from one setting to another. Just let the imagery come and go without censoring it. Then, of all the places you've seen, eventually you will want to pick one that has the most appeal to you. It should be an imaginary location that does not exist in actuality. This is important, because if you choose a place you have been before, you will bring preconceived ideas about it when you go there. Though this isn't necessarily wrong, I believe that it is better to choose a place that has no history attached to it.

Once you have chosen a place that feels right to you, it will remain the same in all the rest of your meditations. However, in each of the following meditations, you will discover more and more details about it. Eventually, it will become completely fleshed out in your mind, with length, width, and depth. Once it has, it will become a very magical and private place where miracles occur.

In this particular meditation, you will begin to feel the resonance of safety by letting in the love of all your unseen friends. They will speak to you in your mind. There is no reason for you to try to see them. Therefore, when we get to that part, just close your mental eyes and listen. It is perfectly all right to make it up and just pretend. You do this by allowing your inner voice to tell you the kinds of things your unseen friends might say to you. The more you can allow yourself to be embraced by their love, the more you will feel. This is true even if you think you have made the whole thing up.

If you will allow yourself to feel your feelings, this meditation will have tremendous impact on you. Feeling your feelings is the key to all your healing, and the more you can feel, the more quickly you will heal. As you allow in the positive feelings of love and safety, perhaps feelings you have never really felt before, you will begin to grow, to change, and to evolve at an accelerated rate. Because your desire for love will be quickened, this single meditation, though simple, can have a wonderful healing effect. This meditation will also prepare you for all the other meditations in this book, because all the rest of them begin and end at the safe place.

The Meditation

Say your induction, replacing the words "meeting your Beloved" with "going to discover your safe place." This will give your subconscious the proper cue it needs to take you there. Also, remember to speak slowly if you are taping this meditation yourself. You will know in a few minutes after entering trance if you have taped it too quickly. If that's the case, go back to the drawing board and do it again more slowly. You will probably only make that mistake once, and all the rest of the meditations will be easy. This particular meditation should take you about twenty minutes to do. Three or four dots after a word indicate places where you should tape silently for a few moments to give yourself time to do what the words indicate.

Find yourself there now, in your safe place, at your favorite time of day, and open up your senses one by one.... See the colors first, the blue of sky, the greens and golds of grass or trees.... Let each color take shape as the earth tones and the water tones become the landscape all around.... Let yourself discover your safe place. Imagine it with your heart or with your mind, or just pretend, if that is what you call it. Let your safe place expand, detail by detail.... Is it a forest clearing or an ocean beach? Perhaps you will find yourself at the side of a lake, or standing by a bubbling brook. Or maybe it's a meadow you stand on, with wildflowers all around. Perhaps your safe place is the top of a high mountain, or the sandy floor of a painted desert with its red and orange hues. Let the pictures come and go until you find one that, for some unknown reason, speaks to you more than all the rest and then fasten your attention there.... Just look, with curiosity, to see what you will find.... (Tape silently for at least 90 seconds to give yourself a chance to discover your safe place.)

Sense the sounds that one might hear in this safe place ... the cry of birds, the rustle of leaves. Listen to the quiet, the hushed stillness, the expectancy of this safe place ... whatever is there that is appropriate to hear.... Then smell the fragrance of your safe place ... what is that scent carried on the breeze? Earth smells or water smells? Smell the safety.... Then touch the safety. Let it fill you up with its love. There is nothing that can harm you here. No stinging insects, no plants with thorns. Touch the safety with your whole being and with your heart.... Reach out a hand and feel what is there — the bark of a tree or cool of a rock. Let the sand or soil sift through your fingers. Do whatever is appropriate for you to do in your safe place.... Then taste the safety. Breathe it deeply into your lungs — fresh clean air. Open your nostrils and feel the air streaming in. Feel the awe as you tilt back your head to breathe it in and to embrace the safety of this safe place....

Let your feelings well up within you and shout them out to all the world, "I am here! I am here! This is my safe place and I am so glad to be here!" Touch, taste, and feel the safety with your whole being. Give yourself permission to have it all. You can have it all.

Feel the love that surrounds you here; let it envelop you. Let your mind open up and be forever free.... Let it in, let it in ... the love of all your unseen friends is here today. Let them hold you in their love.

Perhaps it occurs to you that your angels are everywhere, everywhere ... twinkling on the breeze, watching silently in the air. Your angels are here and they want to give their love to you. Let them hold you to their hearts. Give yourself permission to open up and receive their love for you. Let them whisper in your inner ear ... "We love you. We love you so much. We are here for you. Open up all your senses and rise into the resonance of our safety. Give yourself permission to have it all. Open up your senses and feel your feelings. Let it in, dear one, let it in. This place is for you. It is our gift to you, the gift of purest love, sparkling diamond-like in the sun. Let us heal you with our love. Let us shine our light upon you and raise you into the vibration of our love. Let us raise you up to us. We love you so. You have no idea how glad we are that you came here to be with us today. Let us touch you and hold you with our love. Peace, my child, peace. We are with you now."

Listen now, with your own inner ear and see what more they have to say to you. Let them talk to you. (Tape silently for two minutes so that you can listen to them speak.)

And you talk to them and tell them of your love. (Tape silently for two minutes to give yourself time to respond.)

They are here. They are truly here. Let yourself have the resonance of their safety....

And in a moment you will open your eyes. Your eyes will open on the count of five and not before. One, coming all the way back into your body. Two, becoming aware of your external environment. Three, wiggling fingers and toes. Four and five, open your eyes. Back in the room, awake, alert, alive, refreshed and oh, so loved.

This meditation to find your safe place can and should be done several times before you begin the next meditation, which is a more direct approach to the Beloved. After your safe place is vividly established in your mind, it will not take nearly as long to go there and climb into the resonance of safety. The land formations will already be set and will not shift and change in your mind. You will know what to expect and you will find what you found before. Except for the fluctuations in nature, time of day, and season that will be discovered brand new in each meditation, your safe place will basically always be the same.

With each of the following meditations, you will still need to take the time to firmly establish yourself in the safety even after you've been there hundreds of times. Discovering the sensory details will put you very deep into trance, which is an important precursor to whatever work you want to do in your meditation. Also, the imagery that you found in your safe place is very specific and unique to you, so don't question why you chose what you chose. Every rock and flower, tree or stream has a reason for being there. You may not know the reason for a long time. Eventually, however, you will discover why you chose what you chose. For now, just let it be. Revel in it. It is yours!

191

If you did not experience much of anything in this first meditation, just let it be. You are not a failure, and neither is the meditation. Many people have difficulty visualizing and feel a great deal of anxiety around it. There were those of us who were punished for "daydreaming" as children, and nowhere in our society have we been encouraged to dream. Therefore, if you found it difficult, cuddle up to your inner child and tell them that it's all right. Eventually, you will have vivid pictures. For now, however, you are here to just explore the fun and adventure of learning how to do it.

If you went numb in your meditation, that is fine too. No one said that you should be perfect in your first experience of meditating. It may take a while to undo years of negative conditioning around both dreaming and feeling, so give yourself permission to take as long as it takes. After you've done this meditation two or three times, you might be surprised to discover yourself beginning to thaw.

Some of you may have actually felt fear around the idea of so many celestial beings watching you. We have been so negatively conditioned in our society by horror movies and ghost stories that some of us actually fear the idea of spirit beings. If you watched horror movies when you were a child or adolescent, you can be sure you carry residual fear from this experience. Even though your logical adult mind may tell you there is nothing to be afraid of, there may be a child or adolescent in you that knows the truth: spooks are scary and can't be trusted. At least that is the truth as they see it, and therefore, it is true for you. If this is how your child or adolescent feels, give them a voice and let them speak. As you listen to their comments — quietly and without judgment — you can become conscious of inner beliefs you did not know you had.

To resolve this problem you can simply hold your inner child lovingly. Then tell them that at no time will the adult you not be in control of your meditations. At any moment, if things get too frightening, you can simply open your eyes. Then assure them that you will never let any harm come to them as you do your inner work. This should be enough to put them at ease. Please review the chapter entitled "Healing the Inner Child and Adolescent" for further instructions on how to do this.

You may have experienced great emotion during this meditation. That is because most of us are hungry for the touch of spiritual love in our lives. We live in a society with upside-down values that preaches its lies to us on every TV show, in every movie, on every billboard, and in every advertisement we see. We are ravenous for spiritual touch. We long to be touched by that which is real, and there is a part of us that still remembers the truth no matter how dim the memory may be. Only love is real, and the only place it can truly be experienced is within. In the world within, you have nothing to gain, and nothing to give, but love. As you journey with your Beloved, you will be filled with the vibrations of "inner" love and you will begin to have an appreciation for that which is eternal. It is here that your cup will be filled and you will drink the Divine.

Meditation 2

Hearing Your Beloved's Voice

In this next meditation I will take you to meet your Beloved,
but you will not yet see them in form. That won't occur until
the following meditation called Transcending the Veil, and
even then you may not see them. You can still begin to get a sense
of your Beloved, however, which is what this meditation is designed
to help you do. Also, you will begin to hear their voice, much like
you did in the last meditation when you heard the voices of your
unseen friends.

After you have gone to your safe place and experienced it
detail by detail, you will rise into the resonance of safety by hearing
your angels speak to you. Then you will turn your attention toward
your Beloved. Once you do, you will tell them how much you long
for them and how much you desire them to be in your life.

At a certain point in your dialogue you will realize that,
although you are the one who is speaking, it is their vibration that
has come into your voice, and they are using their vibration and

your words to speak to you. At this point, this is the only way you are capable of hearing them. You must use your longing as a catalyst. Don't be ashamed or embarrassed by this or think it is silly. Since they are your inner voice that loves you, you access them through longing and desire. Since they exist in the vibration of love, the only way that you can get to your Beloved is through deep emotion. The more genuine emotion you can feel, the more they will respond to you. Therefore, tell them from the depths of your soul how much you want and need them.

Whatever you do, however, remember to always tell them the truth. They recognize lies immediately. It is better to be honest and genuine than to try and feel feelings that you do not yet have. If you are not certain you want them in your life or don't believe they are real, tell them this instead. However, do it with deep emotion. They will respond to anything that you say to them from the heart. They will not respond to you at all if what you say to them comes from cold and calculating intellect. When you do this meditation with honesty and depth of emotion, it can be a very intimate experience if you allow it to be. By remembering that your Beloved is real and that they care deeply about you, you will be able to approach this meditation with the attitude that will create success. This meditation will take about twenty minutes to do.

The Meditation

Begin with the same induction as before, only this time, change the words in the beginning to, "And now, to begin the journey to meet your Beloved and hear their voice."

Find yourself there now, in your safe place, at just the right time of day, and open up your senses one by one.... See the colors first, the blue of sky, the green or gold of grass or trees. Let each color take shape as the earth tones or the water tones become the landscape all around.... Imagine it with your heart, or just pretend if that is what you call it. Let these colors and shapes meld into a picture — a picture of safety, a picture of peace. Let it expand, detail by detail, growing into a symphony of color, shape, sound, fragrance, and feeling.... And, as it takes on form, sense the sounds that this safe place might make — perhaps the lap of waves or the chatter of a squirrel. Feel the hush — the hush and rhythm of safety.... Listen to the quiet ... then smell the fragrance of your safe place.... Catch the scent carried in the air. Breathe it deep into your lungs. Feel your nostrils expand as they inhale the safety.... Then taste the safety. Roll it around on your tongue and swallow it, deep into the inner core of your being.... Then touch the safety. Touch ... touch the safety with your whole being and with your heart. Reach out with hand or toe and feel the textures and the temperature of safety ... feel the warmth on your brow or a tender breeze. Let yourself be caressed by the safety....

Feel the love that surrounds you here — let it envelop you. Let your mind open up and be forever free as you feel the love surrounding you. Let it in, let it in ... the love of all your unseen friends, your angels and guides. Remember their love, loving you. Feel the gratitude and the grace. Tell them how much you love them. Rise into the resonance of their safety. (Tape silently for one minute to give yourself time to verbalize your love and gratitude for your unseen friends.)

And now turn your attention to your Beloved. Feel the sudden hush pour through you as you catch your breath in anticipation. Your Beloved is here. Think on this for awhile. They wait for you here, in gentle vibration, in the quiet solitude of their love. Close your eyes and let yourself be very still as you listen — listen for the sounds of their love.

With eyes still closed tight, tilt your head back and focus your whole attention on your inner sensing. Feel the longing. Allow yourself to long for them as never before. Let this longing bubble up into your throat and spill over into your voice and speak your words of longing to them. They have the ears to hear. Tell them of your love for them. "I love you," you might say. "I long for you with my whole heart and whole soul. I want you so much. I want to be with you. I need you so." Express your desire with abandon. Say the words you so need to say, and do that now. (Tape silently for two minutes as you give yourself time to speak.)

Now, as you speak, without missing a beat, realize that it is they who speak to you. Using your voice, they need to say, as hungrily as you, the same words you speak to them. Let them tell you of their desire. "I need you. I want you so. I have waited so long for you to come to me...." Open up your inner ear and let them talk to you. "I love you. I want you. You are my Beloved and I claim you as my own." (Tape silently for three whole minutes to give them time to speak. Make it up and just pretend. What would a Beloved say to you if they were real?)

Feel your feelings. Let them all come up unrestrained. Cry out your love, your longing, your desire. Still with eyes closed, feel their arms go all around you. Let them envelop you in their love....

They have longed to touch you for an eternity. Surrender to their love. Surrender to their embrace. Let them fill you with the vibrations of their loving thoughts, their words, their hunger and passion for you. Let them tell you that there is nothing you can do to change eternal love. There is no way that you can turn their love away from you. Let them hold you to their heart. Let them touch you with the vibrations of their love. You can have it all. You can have it all.

And in a moment you will open your eyes. Your eyes will open, on the count of five and not before. One, coming all the way back into your body. Two, beginning to sense the room around you. Three, wiggling fingers and toes. Four and five, open your eyes, back in the room, awake, alert, alive, refreshed, and oh, so loved.

Meditation 3

Transcending the Veil

I n the next meditation you will see your Beloved in physical
form. You will go to your safe place and rise into the resonance of safety by greeting your unseen friends. Then, you
will remember your Beloved and try to see them. All you will be
able to see is a muted light and an indistinguishable form, however,
because they will be standing behind a veil.

As you look at their light you will begin to ponder the difference between the two of you and begin to feel all of your feelings.
You can allow every feeling you have about yourself as a fallible
human being to come up, as well as feelings about the nature of
the Divine. In this meditation, it is especially important to get in
touch with your contracting emotions, your anger or rage at having
to be physical in the first place. Also, really feel your shame, fear,
loneliness, hurt, despair, or hopelessness. If you can, creatively
make these feelings bigger, shouting them out with abandon and
drama. In order to get to the light, you must first go through the

dark. By feeling your contracting emotions first, you give your unconscious mind a symbolic representation of what you are trying to achieve. Therefore, be creative and give yourself permission to have your pain, censoring nothing.

The more honest you can be with yourself, the more you can allow your feelings to come up uncensored, the greater impact this meditation will have on you. This is the time to let your cruel and vicious inner voice speak, the time to be hateful, arrogant, and hostile. Give yourself permission to cry or rage or be mean and belittling. Or give yourself permission to be numb if that is all you feel. Then let your inner voice talk about how stupid you are to feel nothing. The important thing is just to say something. Once you activate this voice, you may find that it will take on a life of its own and you can't shut it up. This is the goal — to activate what is within so it can be brought to the surface and given a voice. Once this has occurred you are halfway home.

After you have felt all these feelings, your Beloved will call to you. Although you will hesitate, eventually you will go to them. Because of your emotions and the glare of the light, your eyes will still be closed. Then you will give them your voice and they will talk to you in much the same way as in the previous meditation. Afterward you will talk to them, telling them all your long-hidden feelings of longing and desire. Then, you will use your body as an antenna to discover them through your senses, until you eventually open your eyes and, hopefully, see them in form. Their image may come and go, or you may just get little snatches of imagery and be unable to see them as an entire picture. What is hoped for, more than the ability to see them, is the ability to sense them. Whatever occurs is acceptable.

As time goes on and you interact with your Beloved, their form will eventually coalesce into what would be, for you, the epitome of love. This will all come in its right time, so do not fear. Whatever happens is exactly what is supposed to happen. If you give yourself permission to have it all, all will be given to you, including the ability to accept yourself exactly as you are right now. I think you will find this meditation to be quite revealing and deeply moving. If you allow it to be all that it can be, it will be more than you ever expected. My best wishes go with you on this particular journey, because it is a meditation of deepest love. For the best results, it needs to be taped using your most expressive voice and long pauses when it is time to speak or listen.

The Meditation

Begin with the Induction, except the opening words should say, "And now to meet your Beloved and transcend the veil...."

Find yourself now in your safe place at just the right time of day, opening your senses, one by one.... See the colors first, the blue of sky, the greens and golds of grass or trees. Let each color take shape as the earth tones and the water tones become the landscape all around.... Let yourself discover your safe place detail by detail, ever new but always just the same. Imagine it with your heart or with your mind, or just pretend if that is what you call it.

Notice first the time of day. Is it early morning or dawn or dusk, or is the sun gentle and warm upon your face? Or darkest night with a thousand twinkling stars, in this, your safe place?... And now the weather and the season: What time of year would it be? Is it cool or hot, or are the leaves turning colors on the trees? Are there clouds in the sky or do a thousand flowers spread their colors on the ground nearby?...

What sound might you hear in this safe place? Listen with your heart. Do you hear the hush, the quietness of safety all around?... Smell the fragrance of your safe place. What is that omnipresent scent in the air? Earth smells, water smells. Smell the safety.... Touch the safety. Let it fill you with its love. Reach out a hand or toe and feel what there is to feel. No stinging insects, no plants with thorns, no poisonous snakes. Touch, touch the safety of this safe place.... Taste the safety.... Breathe it deeply into your lungs — fresh clean air, cool or warm. Open your nostrils and feel the air streaming in. Feel the awe as you tilt back your head to breathe it in. This is your safe place and nothing can harm you here.

As you let the love surround you, let yourself remember your unseen friends. Open your heart and speak out your love to them. Feel the gratitude. The joy. The peace. Rise into the resonance of their safety. Feel their eyes watching you, their hearts loving you. Open up and let it in. Your angels, they are everywhere.... (Silent taping for one minute as you listen to or think about the love of your unseen friends.)

Now a hush, hush. A quiet vibration enters in. Your senses become poised, alert as you remember: Your Beloved is here.... Look around you now. Out of the corner of your eye, your attention is drawn to a light — over there, no just over there.... As you turn your head to look, you see a shrouded figure in white standing there, but without details. And there they are. You look but can't quite see ... because they stand behind a veil of thinnest gauze. It mutes the light, but even from your side of the veil perhaps you realize that their light must be very bright indeed because even the veil cannot completely hide it....

You look to them across this distance and feel — feel what? There they are, a celestial being too lovely to behold. And here you are, just a human, limited and ugly in your form. How could they possibly want you? The distance between you seems so great. And then you feel your loneliness, pain, shame, or guilt. And all the ugliness you know is within comes spilling out. Your ugly body, your mistakes, your meanness, and all the wrongs you ever did. They rise to the surface and scream at you. Though its voice is hideous you let it speak. "I am ugly, I am stupid, just plain no good." Or perhaps it says, "You are too good for this, what on earth are you doing here? This is ridiculous." Just listen to that voice and let it talk to you. (Silent taping for three minutes as your inner vicious voice talks to you about your human failures.)

As you feel your feelings, you melt in shame. "My God," you think, "nowhere to run, nowhere to hide." You sink down, covering your head with your arms, you try to hide yourself but you know that it's too late — the lies, your unloving thoughts, your rages and your shame, they have all been revealed. . . .

It occurs to you that your Beloved must not see all those things you have always sought to hide within. And now you cry in shame and rage and pain and build a fortress of shadows around yourself to stay hidden in. The mist of fog floats all about you, dark and bitter. And with each breath it becomes more dense . . . the better to hide you in. (Silent taping for 45 seconds while you watch yourself become enshrouded in dense fog.)

Yet through this dark seemingly impenetrable wall, you hear a distant sound, almost inaudible. Is it a voice? In quiet stillness you choke back your tears and strain to hear. . . . It is speaking to you. It says: "My Beloved, I wait for you. I long for you. I need you so. My arms are empty without you. I long to comfort you and hold you. There is nothing you have ever done that could turn my love away from you, no deed that is too dark or terrible that I cannot heal for you. Come to me. Come to me, my love. I desire you to be with me. I want you so." Let them speak to you now. Give them your voice and let them speak words of comfort and desire into your inner ear. (Silent taping for three minutes while they speak to you.)

Now you turn to them. You see that the shadows you have wrapped around you are but a dark mist. And as you see it for what it is, it disappears.... You look to your Beloved where they stand, shrouded in light. There is but one more veil that stands between you. Slowly you get up off the ground. With your eyes locked upon the figure, you hear their voice say, "Come to me. Come to me. I need you so...."

And so you take a step, and then another, until you can reach out and just touch that veil, and on the other side, your Beloved reaches out and touches you. You feel or sense their fingers on your finger tips now, and you feel the longing go through you.... In one mad rush, you don't care anymore. You don't care about all the shame and all the ugliness within. You want them so! You reach out your hands to them and, quickly, they reach out to you and pull you in, across the veil, and into their arms you go.

And all at once you feel them, their arms, their breath, their warmth. With eyes still shut tight against the glare you cry out your pain and your longing against their breast. "I want you so. I need you. Never let me go." Tell them now all that you need to say. (Silent taping for three minutes.)

As you talk, they cradle you, and rock you back and forth. And now, with tears all spent, you become very aware of their presence. Using your body as an antenna, you sense them, first with your heart and then with your mind. Are they soft and feminine, or masculine and strong?...And just how high does your head fall upon their chest, or does yours rise above theirs?...Can you feel their hands?...Do their fingers caress your face?...Do their arms entwine you tightly in their love, or is it a gentler, softer embrace?...

What are they wearing? Can you sense the texture of their clothes?... Now you begin to really wonder: Just what do they look like?... As you gather in all this information, you step back at arm's length ... but still holding hands, you open your eyes to gaze into their face.... Perhaps you can see it in detail, or perhaps not, or perhaps little snatches of imagery come and go.... In any case, you sense their eyes gazing deeply into yours. It is this you focus your attention on, and as you look, you see within them the boundlessness of their grace. Two pools of deep compassion and desire look into yours.... You step back into their arms, and they say to you, "I love you so. Never leave me, my Beloved. I've waited so long to hold you. Stay with me. I will never let you go!..."

And on and on you commune with them. You don't know for how long. But in a moment you know it will be time to go. Now make your promises to each other to return and meet again.... (Silent taping for one minute to give yourself time to say your good-byes.)

And to their world they must go, and you to yours. Yet you know, in your heart of hearts, that you will never be alone again. Not really, for the veil has been parted and your Beloved has ushered you within.

And now a final kiss and an embrace. It's time to say goodbye.

And in a moment you will open your eyes. Your eyes will open on the count of five, and not before. One, coming all the way back into your body. Two, becoming aware of your surroundings. Three, wiggling fingers and toes. Four and five, open your eyes. Back in the room, awake, alert, alive and refreshed and oh, so loved.

This meditation has far-reaching effects and can be done many times in many different applications other than seeing your Beloved in physical form. You can use it anytime you feel wrapped up in your pain or root emotion. If you are feeling the loneliness of your pain and you desire to transform it, you can do this meditation, feeling all your feelings, giving that which is perhaps not desirable in you a voice, and letting it speak. When you sincerely go to your Beloved and tell them you are ready to give this aspect of yourself up, they will hear and they will answer. They know the desires of your heart and they are here to give you your heart's desire. Unfortunately, you don't always know your heart's desire; this is where the problem arises.

Transcending the veil into the light means you are ready to give up all your darkness. Your darkness is simply that which hides the light in you. It is your pain, your shame, and your need to manipulate and control in order to get love. Your darkness contains the secrets you keep hidden even from yourself because it is too terrible to look at. As these "secrets" are revealed to you and you become truly ready to give them up, you can do this meditation and enter into the light with your Beloved. At this point, the light will not be just a metaphor to you. It will be the only truth you know and all you ever wanted.

The effects of this meditation will never end. Not only does it trigger your conscious mind to remember the truth about you, it is a powerful stimulus for your subconscious and unconscious to do the work needed to heal you. Each time you do it, you will feel closer to your Beloved, and the intimacy generated by each encounter will serve to motivate you to continue your healing work.

You can do this meditation as many times as you like. You will probably find that the experience will be different each time, as well as the words you say to them and they to you. I encourage you to do this meditation several times because it carries with it a special resonance that holds, within it, the heart of heaven. It is a special gift to you from my Beloved and me.

If you were unable to see your Beloved in form, this is not important. The important part is feeling your feelings and sensing the presence of your Beloved. If this is all you are ever able to do in meditation, this is enough and will suffice. Although seeing form is not important, it does add interest and you can gather much information from visual cues. However, sensing and feeling are far more important than visualizing will ever be, because it is in sensing and feeling that the impact lies. This impact is what will cause you to experience the changes you want to make in your life and then to heal.

If you didn't see, sense, or feel, this is exactly what was appropriate for you. Your Beloved does not expect you to be perfect, and neither should you. Your willingness and motivation to undergo the meditation and try to see, sense, and feel that which our culture has never encouraged us to experience is enough of a sign to your Beloved that you are trying to contact them. If you sincerely desire to be with them, they will know of this desire and will take the steps necessary for you to sense them in other ways, as long as you remain open to receiving inner guidance.

The trance work I am describing is certainly not the only way to find your Beloved. Trust your Beloved to know the way that's best for you. They may lead you in what seems to be a circuitous route, but if you need this, don't question it. You may need to experience other metaphysical literature first or particular teachers before you can meditatively visualize in this way. Give yourself permission to do this. Eventually, you will be able to meditate, to sense, feel, and even see them, for this is your right as a Divine child, as your Beloved's Love.

If an inability to visualize, sense, or fantasize is your problem, my advice to you is to stay closely connected to your feelings and be as honest as you possibly can. You must ask yourself what part of you is afraid to do these things, and give that aspect of yourself a voice. Let it talk for as long as it needs to, without judgment. Many of us have been programmed to believe that fantasy and visualization are wrong or demeaning. As you allow these beliefs to rise to the surface, you can logically transform them through your new-found wisdom. Then, gently and lovingly, tell this voice that you understand its concerns but that you have now chosen a different path for your life.

You can even personify this voice in form, as discussed in the chapter on symbolic imagery, and deal with it in this way. As you tell it, in no uncertain terms, that no one has a right to control your life but you, its interference will decrease. The power of decision is your right. If used wisely, it will turn the entire pattern of your life around. By using this technique, you can free yourself from your ego's influence forever.

Indeed, the power of decision is the only real power we have left to us as beings who have chosen to live in a dark world where the truth has been kept hidden. You are not your ego, and you need to decide unequivocally that it does not rule your life. Otherwise, it will. If you decide instead to be one with the truth in you and not with the lies, the light will become your guide for decision-making and you will create much more harmonious conditions for both yourself and the world.

Eventually, in doing the previous meditation and in your life as well, you will see that the dark fortress you have made around yourself, which has always seemed so solid, is nothing but mist and can be transcended easily as you choose to step into the light. Here, you will be greeted by your Beloved, and your heart's desire will be made apparent to you. You will see your Beloved and your heart's desire, and you will know the truth. From then on, you will go into meditation wide-eyed with expectancy, and you will not be disappointed.

Meditation 4

Setting the Intent to Change

In the following meditation you will set the intent to change by making a conscious decision to see things differently. In it, you will go to your safe place and tell your Beloved that you are ready to change. Then you will give your Beloved your voice so they can speak to you. They will tell you that you create your reality through your beliefs and that in order for you to have external change, you must change internally first.

After this, they will take you out of the safety. You will walk on a pathway to a swamp. The more you can see, sense, and feel, the better. Make it up and just pretend. See the path and the logical landscape you would naturally see. Feel your Beloved's hand in yours, leading you. Involve your whole body in the experience. Let your left brain remind you of what would logically be there, and allow your right brain to create the feelings and sensations of walking in and experiencing your environment.

When you get to the swamp, it will be a slimy, ugly, muddy

place. Feel all your feelings of revulsion and disgust. At a certain point, the mud will form itself into a human shape that will be a personified representation of your resistance to change. Allow yourself to discover what kind of human being the mud becomes — man or woman, child or gruesome beast. They can become someone from your past or someone unknown to you. You may end up either feeling attracted to them or they may be repulsive to you.

I always visualize my ego as a very handsome and seductive man. Because my ego is an energy that I have willingly united with since I began my journey into physicality, my unconscious mind has chosen to show it to me in this way. When it does, I get a very clear message about why I am choosing not to change. Until I realize that my ego seduces me with empty lies that lead to pain, I will never see things differently and choose a more productive way.

You may or may not have the same kind of visual experience I have. If you do, it is important that you allow yourself to feel the attraction, and even make it bigger. Allow yourself to be seduced. Then, when it comes time to say "no" to it, do it with gusto. Put all the power of your choice and decision into your voice and let the creature, created out of the mud, know in no uncertain terms that you recognize its lies and that you will not be seduced by it again.

Through the intensity of your emotions, you will go very deep into trance. The deeper you go, the more insight this meditation will give you. The more you can feel, the more real it will be. The more real it is, the more you will convince your unconscious mind that you really do want to change. Since you create the majority of your reality from unconscious beliefs, changing its mind will have massive impact on what occurs in your life.

If you are honest in this meditation, you will change. Though you may still not understand how to receive guidance, information will come trickling in. You will begin to have the sense that your Beloved is with you all the time, and that there is no hardship the two of you cannot face together. Though the learning may come slowly, with each advancement in your progress, your motivation to change will be renewed. Once this occurs, you will receive the miracle of a healed perception that will allow you to shift quickly into higher consciousness. Therefore, let go of your fears. Lay them down in quiet certainty, knowing that your Beloved has come to be your guide and to take you home to your heart's desire, where you belong.

If you are taping this meditation yourself, be sure to include, in the induction, a few words about going on a journey to create the intent to change by allowing your Beloved to be your guide. Speak with feeling, and give yourself adequate pauses to respond at the appropriate places. This meditation should take you about forty-five minutes to do.

The Meditation

First, do the induction of your choice.... Five ... four ... three ... two ... one....

Sense yourself there now, in your safe place, at the perfect time of day.... Sense the colors first, the blue of sky, the greens and golds of grass or trees. Let the colors become the landscape all around — the earth tones, the water tones, rich browns or variegated shades of gray. See all things visible that are here today and notice how they sparkle with an inner light, just a bit more vibrant than when you were here before.... And if it's a sunny day, notice how the sun lights up the sky and how it seems to be watching you. Does it shine a bright and golden orb of light nestled in a sky of deep, deep blue?... Just look and see what there is to see in this safe place today....

Feel it now.... Feel the sunlight upon your brow or face, and notice how it dazzles before your eyes.... Or feel the cool against your cheek.... Is there a breeze, or is it a warm and sultry day where the itch of sweat trickles down your cheek?... Feel your body here. Use it as an antenna. Sense the sensations of your safe place.... Touch, taste, see, smell, hear — let all the sensations come flooding in.

Sense the safety. No stinging bees, no poisonous snakes, no plants with thorns or toxic resins, no wild beasts. Only the hush and the resonance of safety, all around. Let it in. Let it in....

Now, looking around you once again, you know that your Beloved is near. You feel their presence very acutely. Perhaps you call to them in your mind. Where are you my Beloved? I want to see you so. And somewhere, within the safety, they appear. Imagine it or just pretend. Even though you may not see the details of their face or form as yet, know that they are there. Perhaps you see them first beside a tree or in a clearing, or perhaps as a faint ball of light that floats down from the sky and lands before you and shimmers before your sight.

You look at them, perhaps feeling shy, remembering the last time you were here and all the love you shared. Now you step forward and look into their eyes, and you feel them calling you in your mind. "Come to me, my Beloved. I want you so." And now you rush to them, and into their arms you go. Feel their warmth all around you in a wonderful embrace of love and care. And in your heart of hearts, you know that they are as glad to see you again as you are to see them. Perhaps you think to yourself, "I am wanted. I am loved. I need never be afraid again." Let it in. Let it in — the peace and the wonder of your shared love with them.

With that, you remember the reason why you are here today. You know it is time for you to change. You've had enough of loneliness, enough of blame. You don't want it anymore. It has been a long and weary road you have traveled, and you are longing to go home to the peace of your Beloved's arms and the safety of their embrace.

Now you look into their eyes and see the stillness there. They look back at you with such gentleness, silently encouraging you to speak. At first hesitant, you don't quite know how to start. Perhaps, in a tiny voice or blurting it out all at once, you say to them: "I'm ready to change. I'm ready to give up the ways of the world, only I don't know how because it's all I've ever known. I've been here so long, I grew up learning how to blame. It scares me to think about changing. I'm afraid I will have no defenses against attack. I don't know what to do, but I know that I want you, and in order to have that, I'm willing to do anything you want me to do."

Talk to them now, using your own words, and tell them about your desire to see things differently, even though you don't understand how. (Continue taping silently for ninety seconds.)

They look to you with such love in their eyes and suddenly you know that everything is going to be all right. Perhaps they hold you just a little tighter to show you how much they care. Perhaps you let them lift, for you, all your burdens that are too heavy for you to bear.

They look into your eyes now and smile with confidence and say, "I can take your pain from you. It is not too heavy for me. Give it to me, my Beloved. Let me heal you. Through the power of our belief and our shared love there is nothing we cannot do together and, by the same token, nothing either of us can do alone. So together we will fight your foes and vanquish them. Have no fear. We will succeed. As you give me your little willingness I will take it and meld it into a powerful intent that will turn any darkness into light. It is only your belief that stands in our way. It takes but a decision to change it. We can do it together." Now let them talk to you in your mind and listen to what they have to say. (Continue taping silently for three minutes.)

You ask them if they will be with you when you fight this foe, and they say, "No, this is the one decision you must make alone; but I will not be far behind and I will give you a gift to help you fight the battle." Now, reaching somewhere into the garment they wear, they pull out a small, black velvet bag with a draw string top, and place it in your hand. You feel its softness as it touches you, but you can't imagine what could be inside that could possibly help you to vanquish your foe. You start to look but they tell you, "No, don't look now. Keep it somewhere on you, ready for later use." You find a pocket or perhaps hang it on your belt. If nothing else, you stuff it in your shirt.

Now they take your hand and tell you to walk with them. You go along a path. Perhaps you never noticed it was there before, but here it is now. As you walk with your Beloved, they tell you they must take you out of safety to meet and do battle with your enemy. The trail begins to wind as you move beyond the borders of safety. You walk into a dark forest with trees and outstretched branches everywhere. You walk and walk, seeing and hearing and feeling whatever is there.... Your Beloved holds your hand and you help each other, perhaps over boulders or logs or around shrubbery.

In this quiet time of travel, your Beloved begins to talk to you about your foe. They tell you that even though your enemy lies waiting, dark and seductive, on the other side of safety, any enemy can be transformed with determination and persistence. All it will take to vanquish your foe is your decision to see things differently and a little willingness to change.

As they talk, your steps wind into uncertainty. You feel a tightness in your gut. The landscape has become very dark as the forest turns into a jungle … and then … a swamp. Dark and oozy things are everywhere. Your feet slide on mud and slime. Branches become claws that grab at you. Your nostrils recoil at the smell of rotting vegetation and the odor of the earth decaying in this wet and watery place. Now you hear the drip and bubble, the gurgle of decay. You look down at your feet; the path you walk upon is sure. It leads you straight into the swamp.

Now your Beloved looks at you and gives you a little shove. "In there," they say, "you will meet your enemy. And don't forget to use the gift I gave thee! Now go!"

You take your little willingness and all the courage you have ever had and walk the path to meet your foe in a swamp of dank, dark, disgusting things.... You don't have far to go, for in the middle of the path rises up a pool of mud, bubbling and gurgling.... It begins to take on human shape....

At first you see two eyes, black holes, and a mouth that drips and smiles at you.... You watch in fascination as this slimy creature takes shape and then reshapes itself again. It seems to have the power to take any form it wants, at times looking dark and ugly … at other times light and fair. Its shape changes back and forth, now this, now that. Perhaps it's a beautiful, voluptuous woman that holds out her hand to you, or a handsome man, strong and virile. Or perhaps it's an innocent child standing there, or someone from your past. It could even be the perfect, but phony, likeness of your Beloved, or it could even be you yourself that you see. Now let it change its shape again, and yet again, until its shape stays sharp, clean, and clear within your mind. And as you watch, they engagingly begin to talk to you....

"Don't listen to that person you were with," they say. "They are just trying to fool you. The world is not your fault. That is ridiculous! It's their fault. It is everyone else who did it to you. Your mother and your father, your lover and your spouse, your teachers, your employer, your so-called friends. They are the ones who do it wrong, who treat you badly, who are inconsiderate of your needs. Not you! You know you always tried your hardest to please everyone. You were innocent. A tiny child, an ignorant youth. How could any of that possibly have been your fault? They were the ones who didn't care, didn't know how to love.

"And all those accidents you had, how could you have caused them? As if you wanted to hurt yourself. That's utterly absurd! Don't be stupid and listen to that rubbish. And what about those aches and pains? Are you going to let them tell you that you caused these too? Come on, everyone knows all about germs and viruses, allergies and genes. Your Beloved is just trying to fool you so you will be the fool instead of them. Don't let them do that to you. They are just tricking you!"

Now give them your voice and let them talk to you and tell you all your doubts, fears, dreads, and everything you have ever believed about the world. (Continue taping silently for three minutes as you listen to them try and seduce you with their lies.)

As they talk, they creep a little closer. You recoil a little, not knowing what to do. In your confusion, you look at them. Don't they speak the truth? They only say the things you've always heard.

How could the whole world be wrong? It must be your Beloved who does not speak the truth. Before you is the most winning smile, engaging and warm, wanting to comfort you. But something about their eyes is as hard as knives and frightens you. "I have money, houses, cars, lots of things," they say. "I can make your body feel really comfortable."

Now you see that they have jewels, lovely clothes, and sweet perfumes. It's obvious that they can take care of you in all the ways you always wanted to be cared for. Now they reach out a hand to you but, in uncertainty, you back away — and suddenly, you remember your Beloved, and all the love and deep compassion in their face. You see them, in your mind's eye, waiting for you to return to them. They look forlorn and all alone.

Now you look at the one who stands before you, so virile or voluptuous, or strong, or stern, or innocent, with a smile upon their face, and all at once you say, "No, no, no. I know the ways of the world. It is not a happy place. There is only pain and sickness, darkness and cruelty there. You can't fool me. You are the one who changes shape and speaks lies. Not my Beloved. The world has never loved me. It offers me its treasures, but they are empty. Hard work and hurting is all I've ever gotten there." Now tell them all you need to say. (Continue taping silently for three full minutes as you tell them about all the promises the world made but never kept.)

As you talk, their shape before you becomes a formless mass of sludge, oozing and bubbling. They begin to creep along the muddy ground toward you. You turn to run, but where? For the first time you notice they are everywhere in this dark, dank, evil place. They stand on every branch, on every limb, in every lane.

In terror you open your mouth to scream, but then you

remember the gift from your Beloved. Quickly, you take out the pouch and, reaching in, you pull out a tiny sphere. Upon your palm you see a little, shining globe of light. It glows both bright and clear. Now you hold it out in front of you and shout with all your might, "No, I will not be fooled by you again."

Now tell them what you must, in no uncertain terms. (Continue taping silently for two minutes as you pour out your outrage at the lies of the world.)

Now, through the Power of your decision, you feel a mighty surge of energy pour through your body and into your hand. Instantly, this tiny sphere leaps into a light so bright and brilliant that all darkness disappears.... Now, within a tiny fraction of a second, within one blink of your eye, you are transported ... entwined in your Beloved's arms, back in your own safe place, the promised land!

Your Beloved looks at you with a smile of purest love and compassion. They say to you, "That's all it takes, my Beloved. A firm decision and a little willingness and the light is everywhere. You and I together, we cannot fail. I with my light and you with your desire to know the truth, we can go anywhere and do anything at all. There is no miracle too big or small that I would not give to you to heal you from all your dark and painful thoughts. You will see. Give me your willingness and with you I will always be."

Now say your last good-byes and any final words that need to be said.... Then let them hold you all the way out of trance to the count of five.

In a moment you will open your eyes. You will open your eyes on the count of five, and not before. One, beginning to come back into your body now. Two, sense your environment around you. Three, beginning to wiggle fingers and toes. Four and five, open your eyes. Welcome back, and welcome to the journey home to your heart's desire, where love abides.

Meditation 5

Initiation: the Sword of Truth

This next meditation is an unusual one. It is an initiation. In it, you will meet with a unity of beings who are working toward the preservation of our planet. When you meet them, you will make a commitment to become a healer of the earth. They will initiate you into their unity by giving you a sword. This sword will be a sword of enlightenment that will help you to divide the light from the dark so you can discern the truth.

Before you make the commitment to become a healer of the earth, however, you will go through a symbolic purification ritual with your Beloved. Although you will see your flesh purified by fire in a creative and visual way, it will not hurt you. It is merely a symbolic ritual that will communicate your desire for purification to your unconscious mind. If it bothers you to see your flesh purified by fire, then substitute another ritual in its place.

After your flesh has been symbolically purified, you will then be required to make a sacrifice. The sacrifice you make will be something from your past that no longer serves you. Perhaps it will be your blame or your need to control or punish others. Perhaps it will be your need to hang onto failure or self-pity. Perhaps it will be your shame, anger, sorrow or hopelessness that you give up. Whatever it is, you will discover it by looking for a tangible object — a symbol which you need to sacrifice to discern the truth. As you discuss the symbolism of the object with your Beloved, you will gain insight into what it is you need to give up before you can truly claim to be a healer of the earth.

If done with intensity and great emotion, this meditation will have a profound effect on your unconscious mind. By doing it, you will be telling your unconscious mind three basic things: One, you are ready to sever your ties from the past by sacrificing an unproductive behavior that no longer serves you. Two, you are ready to see all things differently by looking past your illusions, to the truth. And three, you are ready to take responsibility for the consequences of past beliefs. By telling your unconscious mind these things, it can assist you with that process miraculously.

Be sure to cue your unconscious mind several times during the induction, telling it that you are going on a journey to become a healer of the earth. This meditation should take about forty-five minutes to do.

The Meditation

Sense yourself now in your safe place, at the perfect time of day. See the colors first: the golds and greens of grass and trees ... a sky of deepest blue ... rocks and mountains, streams or lakes in rich and vibrant hues.... Let the earth tones and the water tones become the landscape all around.... Notice the time of day by discovering how the shadows fall ... and notice the season: notice how it spreads its special colors over all.... Breathe it in, taste it on your tongue, feel it with your hands and feet, the temperature and texture of your safe place. Then hear the special sounds it makes....

This place is real, healed and whole. Nothing is missing. Every detail has been placed just so you can experience it as it is. Let this idea in: This safe place was created for you. It reflects your joy, your wonder, your magic, and your majesty. Let your whole body fill up with the consciousness of this thought. Feel it in your heart and in your gut, all the gratitude and the thankfulness for that which has been given to you. This is your planet, your home, your world. It has been bestowed upon you as a gift, and it was given in reverence, knowing that you would care for it. Feel the honor of being made a caretaker of such a treasure. This is your Earth and it belongs to you. It is a rare jewel of purest love, created so that it could reflect the light to you.

With these thoughts and feelings filling you, look around you now and find a place to lie down, perhaps on a bed of soft grasses, or in the warm impressionable sand.... Feel the sensations all around you — the solidness, the depth, the pressure on your back.... Feel how the earth cradles you and rocks you in her peace.... And looking up, see the world from a different view — the sky, the sun, the clouds all looking down at you.... Feel the love, earth below and sky above, all meeting as a single point of focus within you.... Perhaps your eyes become heavy now as drowsiness enters. The earth holds you in her arms and the wind rocks you. The gentle sun caresses your face as you begin to drift lazily into sleep in this magical place. Not a care in the world, knowing you are safe ... only a deep feeling of trust and peace as your eyes close and you are sound asleep....

And you begin to dream. Perhaps you dream of safety, soft and warm. No harsh noises, nothing to poke or jab, no glare, no disturbance of any kind, just soft and gentle peace as you sink even deeper into the womb of safety.... Then your attention is caught by a sound, a rhythm, a resonance.... As you listen, you realize that you can hear your own heart beating in the stillness, lub dub, lub dub, and it fills you with quiet joy.... And listening still, you hear another sound, lub dub, lub dub, and you realize that it is another heart beating next to yours.... In wonder, you ask yourself, who could that be? I am not alone. It must be my mother's heart beating with my own. As you listen, the heartbeats become synchronized. Two hearts beating as one, a heart within a heart, a flame within a flame ... you focus on the color red and see them beating in their fiery bed.

Now perhaps you feel as if your body were floating down a tunnel. Without a care you let yourself go down, down, down, knowing that you are safe and loved. All the dark passes safely before your eyes. No sharp pointed objects, no piercing screams, no aches or pains of any kind. You gently let the dark go and leave it all behind.

And you land, feet first, in the very center, the heart of Mother Earth. Taking your time you look all about you now.... This is the most magnificent and awesome place you've ever seen. Feel the excitement rise within you as you realize just exactly where you are.

Now you notice that you are on a path and your feet begin to walk. As you go, you take in all the sights and sounds — the blue sky and the emerald earth. Maybe you see a fawn by its mother's side as it dips its head into a pool of water and drinks, or maybe there are birds circling lazily in the sky. See it all.... Feel the resonance of this place.... As you wander lazily on, you wonder what you are doing here, but then you rest assured that all will be revealed to you at the proper time and place. Rounding corners, you pass through valleys or shaded knolls as you go, until you come to a clearing, bowl shaped, with a bordering of trees or mountains or high rocky walls all around.... You stop and stare.... There is a different energy here. You can feel it in your body ... sense it with your heart.

Suddenly, as you watch, this empty place begins to fill with shapes. As if created out of nothing, starry light begins to form, and to shape itself into angels, guides, unseen friends, and more.... In amazement you feel the hush as they look at you....

Not knowing what to do, you just stand there, feeling a little embarrassed perhaps, until one of their crowd steps forth to speak. As they come closer, you see that it is your Beloved, and your heart lights up with joy. Get a sense of their presence now.... Bring them all the way in to your energy field by focusing your whole attention on their resonance.... You look into their eyes as they look into yours and, as you do, you realize that everything is going to be all right, and that you have come to the right place, at the right time, to receive a gift they have for you.

As your Beloved holds your hand, another steps out of the crowd. It is a woman, tall and beautiful, perhaps young, perhaps old. See her now in your mind's eye.... She is dressed in white, from head to toe. She is the spokesperson for the group. She says, "Welcome, we are so glad you finally made it here. We've waited for you for a long, long time. We need you now. You see, we know that you are a healer, and the earth above needs healing like never before. However, before you can begin your task, you need preparation. Therefore we are going to give you a gift, much like a tool, that you can do your healing with. Before you can receive it, you must be purified. We will leave you with your Beloved now, and tomorrow night, just after dusk, we will meet again, to initiate you into the healers of the Earth."

225

Now, one by one, they fade away, until you stand alone with your Beloved, whose arms entwine you now. They look at you and their eyes look so proud. "You and I," they say, "have come a long, long way on our search for truth together. But I must prepare you for what you will receive, for the beings here will take you much quicker down your path than I can take you alone. The Earth needs you now and we must hurry. There is not much time left."

With that, they tell you that you must help them build a fire. "Purification is what is called for here, and there is no faster way than fire. I will prepare your body with herbs and ointments. Do not be afraid. It will not hurt."

Together, you first make a ring of stone. See yourself pick the stones up and make them into a ring.... And then you gather the sticks and twigs and kindling.... The two of you stack it up, layer by layer, and build a glorious fire, hot and intense, a blaze of light against a sky that is dimming into dark....

Now you stand next to your Beloved, and they take herbs and ointments out of the garment they wear and place them on the ground. They look into your eyes and tell you that you must go naked into the flame. In order to heal all your wounds, they must be completely exposed and, through the fire, purified, so that when you re-emerge, you will come forth whole. Are you ready?

The task before you seems immense, but you trust your Beloved with your whole heart. Therefore, you look into their eyes and speak a quiet "yes."

Quickly, they undress you.... You feel all exposed but do not say a word. Your Beloved is intensely involved with the ceremony now. They take the herbs and rub them over you.... You feel the sting of roughened flesh.... Then they open a jar of oil and scoop it onto their fingers. You look into their eyes as they anoint you with soft and gentle hands.... Beginning at your crown, they work their way down to your feet.... Every inch of your flesh now glistens with the anointing, and you feel an inner glow as it begins to penetrate deeply in....

The fire burns hot before you, and is now a dancing blaze of light. You gaze into it mesmerized, watching the flames flicker and dance, seeing the colors.... Your Beloved takes your chin and forces you to look at them.... They look deep into your eyes and tell you, "Do not fear. It will not hurt. When you step in you will take all your pain. When you step out, your pain will be left in there and you will be whole again."

Now, almost in a daze, you take that one awesome step into the heat and into the blaze of the crackling fire that instantly begins to consume your flesh.... You can see it, but it is as your Beloved said, there is no pain. And when your flesh is gone, your bones begin to burn.... And when your bones are gone, only ashes and dust have made their return to the earth from whence they came....

All through the dark and starry night, your Beloved watches over your remains.... Now as the fire burns down to embers and then black coals, your Beloved sees a fiery sun that begins to light the sky, becoming a blood red, crimson orb that paints its colors across the horizon. Focus on that color now. They know that this is the time of your awakening, your rebirth into the light of day. Quickly, but with deliberation, they take a pouch out of their garment.... They empty its contents into their hand.... It looks to be a fine dust or glittery powder.... Where you stood in the fire the night before, they throw this powder, and instantly, as it touches your spirit body, in a twinkling of stars, your physical body begins to take its shape again.... Out of the pit you step, feeling pure and clean and whole as never before.

Your Beloved takes you directly into their arms, not seeming to notice that you are still naked.... They look deep into your eyes and simply say, "I love you from the depths of my soul. I am so proud to be in love with you." Now, without taking their eyes off yours, they dress you again in a pure white garment.... See the color and cut of it. Feel the intimacy of this moment as they dress you in clothing of pure white....

"We still have much work to do before the fall of night," they say, "when you will receive the gift that will help you on your way. Somewhere in this clearing you will find a sacrifice. It's hidden among the rocks or trees or in the grass. You must look for it and bring it back. You must have something to exchange in return for the gift, and it is already here, waiting to be found."

You are surprised. "What kind of sacrifice?" you ask. "You will know when you find it," they say. "It will be the symbol of something that you are willing to give up. The healer's journey requires willingness and determination. Old ideas must fall by the wayside. Old guilt and shame must be set aside and replaced with new values and concepts. Behaviors that do not serve you must be owned and changed. Therefore, the sacrifice you will find will be a symbol of whatever it is that stands in the way of your healing. This is because, in order to heal the earth, you must first heal yourself. Now go and look and bring me what you find...."

Now you search and search in every nook and cranny, behind boulders, under rocks and in the boughs of trees or in piles of leaves or grass.... Just pretend, make it up and be creative in your search.... The sun traverses the sky, and still you look.... Where on earth could such a treasure be? Finally, as the sun is sinking into night, you find it — right there. (You should search for about one minute, feeling all the frustration and anxiety that a futile search brings.)

Pick it up and look at it in detail. Then let it speak to you. What exactly does it have to say? It will tell you about some negative trait that you are ready to give up. . . . If you can't figure it out, it is certain that your Beloved will have ideas that you don't. Therefore, allow yourself to discuss its symbolism with them. . . . (Give yourself at least two minutes to do this.)

After discussing the symbol with your Beloved, who still stands beside the circle of stones you built the night before, your Beloved takes your sacrifice, looks at it, and simply says, "It is good. Now you don't have long to wait."

The night is turning very dark and, as the stars begin to light the sky, your angels, guides, and unseen friends begin to light the ground whereon they stand. . . . One by one, they appear as brilliant balls of blazing light. They take shape and come forth to begin the ceremony to initiate you into the healers of the Earth. . . .

The same woman you saw yesterday steps forth, and your Beloved indicates that you should give her the sacrifice. . . . You do this, and she takes it and holds it in her hands. Now she speaks. "By this sacrifice, you indicate to us that you are willing to give up the past. You know now that it is time to let go of fear and pain and be done with it, and that you don't need it anymore. It is a new dawn and a new day, and a new era is upon the land. Hatred and war are at an end. Strife of every kind becomes undone as you take your neighbor's hand and call them friend. Are you ready to take the oath of full divinity, to accept the final challenge, to shift your perceptions into higher consciousness and see things differently?" You feel all eyes upon you as you quietly but assertively say, "Yes, I am."

Now tell them why you are ready to take responsibility to heal the Earth, to give up blame and to see all things differently. Tell them that you are willing to let go of the past, to own your darkness, and learn your lessons, so that you can find a better way of being in the world. (Silent taping for two minutes while you speak your truth.)

They nod at you, satisfied with your answer. Now they take your sacrifice and lay it in the ashes in the center of the ring of stones where you purified your flesh the night before.... Gathering all around the stones, everyone waits and watches, forming a tight circle of power, acceptance, and love. You watch each one as they step forth, and you acknowledge them in some way as they do....

Now your sacrifice begins to glow.... The earth begins to tremble.... The winds blow, and you feel a sudden tension in the air.... Your Beloved puts their arm around you to reassure you. "It is the birthing pains," they whisper in your ear.... The roar of quiet is all you hear as everyone stands expectantly, focusing their whole attention upon the sacrifice and the transformation that is near.... Now, from the sky, there comes a mighty crack of lightning, and tumbling down upon the ground is an arc of light, intense and brilliant, gleaming and bright.... It lands precisely in the center of the circle upon the sacrifice.... At the instant it strikes the earth, the earth gives a mighty heave and opens to issue forth a vortex of brilliance all its own....

And in the place the sacrifice was, a mighty Angel appears ... huge, so dazzling and bright, it's hard to look.... You cover your eyes, but still they stand, and when you remove your hands from your face, you see that they are looking directly at you.... In their hand they hold a mighty sword.

With its tip, they first touch your head and then your groin, left shoulder, and then right, ending at your heart.... And then they turn the sword around and, taking it by the tip, they hand it to you....

"This is the sword of truth," they say. "It is a sword of discovery. It is not for destruction, torment, and death. It is for discernment, to help you to hear the lies behind the words and the truth behind the lies, so that you can cut quickly to the heart of any conflict and resolve it with wisdom and with love. We place it in your keeping, knowing that it is in good hands. We trust that in any conflict, you will always use it on yourself first to discern your darkness and learn your lessons. Then, in your quest to take responsibility, you will express your truth appropriately and with wisdom, to dispel the conflict and bring it to an end."

Now, in a flash of light, you are blinded and everything disappears.... In an instant, you find yourself lying down, sleeping peacefully, rocked by gentle winds, caressed by the fingers of warmth that come from the sun in your safe place. As your eyes flutter open, you look up into the face of your Beloved.... Their face looks soft and kind, and they have a gentle questioning look in their eyes. You smile at them and speak your truth. "My Beloved," you say, "I am free. I am free, because I know how to take responsibility!"

Now speak your final words to them and let them speak theirs to you.... Then, when you are ready, let them hold you as you move out of trance to the count of five — and this time, let them do the counting....

231

Meditation 6

Rescuing Your Inner Child

This meditation is only a beginning. The ending is up to you. My intent in this meditation is to bring you into contact with your frightened, hurt, or lonely inner child so that you, who are now their authentic inner parent, can rescue, heal, and bond with them.

In this meditation I will take you to the point at which you remember a time when your child needed rescuing. When a memory comes to you, you must watch it as if it were happening now and then do whatever is appropriate to rescue, protect, heal, and bond with your inner child.

You can use any means at your disposal to do this. You can be highly imaginative or totally realistic. If you, as an adult, are still afraid of your childhood abuser, you will want to call in your Beloved to help you and give you strength. They know that protecting your inner child from an abusive adult or sibling is of the highest priority when it comes to teaching your inner child about love. Your Beloved won't hesitate to do whatever they need to do to protect them and keep them safe. They are not hampered by either your fear or your belief system. Therefore, if you, as the adult, feel inadequate to do the task, your Beloved will gladly step in and protect the two of you.

Bonding with the child is of primary importance. If you are unable to receive a memory, you can still imaginatively bond with your child, loving them and reassuring them that they are not alone. If this is all that occurs, your meditation will be a wonderful success. If you feel dislike for your inner child and don't want to bond with them, give yourself permission to have these feelings. Instead of bonding with your inner child, talk to your Beloved about it, express your feelings of hatred, and let them talk to you.

Perhaps a childhood memory doesn't come to you, but frightening adolescent or adult memories do. If this occurs, go with the flow. These memories are coming up for a reason. If your adolescent appears, heal and bond with them. If it's you, as an adult, remembering a frightening or humiliating situation that happened last week or last year, heal and bond with them. The same procedures still apply.

The healing can be anything from right information to elaborate cleansing or protective rituals. If you already work with guides and angels, you can bring them in, as well as your Beloved. Be creative, but don't worry about what you are going to do beforehand. In inner-child work, you already have a loosely developed plan of action: Review the offending scene, rescue, protect, and bond with your inner child, give the shame back to your child's abusers, and heal your inner child by giving them appropriate information and by teaching them that what occurred wasn't their fault. If you let your imagination flow, in the moment, it won't disappoint you and you will leave yourself open for some glorious miracles to occur.

The Meditation

Sense yourself in your safe place, at just the right time of day. Imagine it or just pretend. Use your body as an antenna to sense your safe place. See the colors first, the blue of sky, the greens and golds of grass or trees. Let the colors take shape and become the landscapes all around.... See, hear, taste, touch, and smell your safe place.... Sense the movement, and let the movement turn into sound. Smell the fragrance, the earth smells or water smells, and let the smell turn into taste, a tingle on your tongue, just the hint of sensation.... Sense the solidness of your safe place. Reach out and feel it.... See yourself in the picture.... Sense the season, time of day, and temperature.... Feel the safety, let it in. Feel the love of your safe place....

Now you hear a gentle rustling sound and sense a presence behind you. Perhaps you hear a quiet footstep and turning, see your Beloved standing there. Reaching out a hand to you, they touch your finger tips and slowly draw you in, closer and closer until you feel their chest against yours and sense the steady rise and fall of their breath. With their hand upon your neck or shoulders and arms encircling you, sense the safety. Feel it within you. Perhaps you commune silently with them for a moment, expressing your love and gratitude.... (Silent taping for one minute.)

Then you begin to talk to them about your inner child, telling them all the things you have been learning. It's been a long, long time since you've seem them or cared about them. You didn't know that they still lived somewhere, lost in the catacombs of time and space. It never even occurred to you that perhaps they could be rescued, perhaps even healed of their pain, much less that you could do the rescuing and the healing.

234

Your Beloved concurs with all you say and maybe even adds a few insights of their own. They tell you that they would like to rescue and heal your inner child with you but first you must find your inner child, and the two of you must bond in order to create a relationship of trust. They ask, "Would you like to meet them now? They are here, hiding in your safe place."

"Where?" you say, looking all around. "I don't see them. Are they hiding for a reason? I wouldn't blame them for not trusting me. Maybe they don't even like me. After all, I abandoned them for such a long time. I taught them that their childish imaginings were stupid. I didn't know that every time I belittled myself I was actually belittling and abusing them. I had no idea how much I hurt them by taking on the role of my critical parents or judgmental teachers to hurt and abuse them again and still again. What should I do?" you ask your Beloved. "Can I ever make it up to them?"

Your Beloved assures you that you can, and they tell you that the way to begin is to find them first and then to heal them of their pain. "Now go and look," they tell you, "behind trees or rocks and see if you can't find them here, hiding somewhere within the safety."

As you begin your search, your thoughts begin to haunt you. Looking here and there, you begin to feel remorse and fear. Perhaps they'll never trust you because you've abandoned them just like everyone else has ... (silent taping for a minute or so while you search and muse over what you have done).

As these thoughts toss and turn within your mind, you hear a sound ... perhaps a sound of crying, or a childish voice calling your name. And turning in the direction of the sound, you go toward it and discover where they have been hiding. Don't be surprised if you are no longer in your safe place but are in your childhood home, a bedroom or a favorite hiding place. Get a sense of that place now....

You stand apart from them and look at them. They stare back at you. It has been a long, long time since you have met. You look into their eyes and try to discern their feelings. Are they lonely, hurt, or afraid? Do they feel shame, anguish, longing, or guilt? Ponder this for a few moments while you look, silently, into their eyes. Can you tell if they want you to be with them now? Can they ever possibly love you?

They look at you with huge round eyes, filled with emotion, and say, "You left me. I was alone and crying in the dark and you left me." Now a memory comes to you of a time when your child was afraid, lonely, or abused. Perhaps it's a memory that you are very conscious of, or perhaps it's one that you seem to have forgotten. As this memory comes to you, review it from start to finish, seeing and feeling all the unpleasant details. (Silent taping for two minutes.)

Now see the revulsive scene again, but this time, step in at the critical moment to rescue your child, telling the abusers exactly what you think of them. Do whatever needs to be done to make your child feel safe. Be creative. Just pretend, but do it with emotional intensity. (Silent taping for three minutes.)

Now that your child is safe, bond with them, telling them it wasn't their fault. Re-educate them, help them understand the ways of the world and say whatever is appropriate to sooth their fears and reduce their sense of humiliation, shame, abandonment, rejection, and betrayal. (Silent taping for three minutes.)

Now it's time for a healing ritual. Think of some ritual that will cleanse your child of their inner pain and visualize doing it with them. Perhaps it will be a cleansing bath, an anointing, magic potions, an experience of Light. Be creative. Be magical.

Now say your final goodbyes, reassuring your child that you'll be back again, then count yourself all the way out of the trance to the count of five.

Meditation 7

The Journey to the Beloved

This meditation is an epic journey. It is much like a parable because it tells a story as you go. It will give you an overview of the spiritual journey and describe the key ingredients to make it a success. It begins, as always, in your safe place, but it ends on a mountain top.

In this meditation you will do what is called a split-off technique. You will watch your spirit self leave your body to go and be with your Beloved. For a time, your consciousness will reside with your spirit self. Later on, it will come back into your body so you can resume the journey. This is a valuable technique because it allows you to see things in a completely different way than before. Have fun with it and accept it for what it is.

You will be sent two guides to help you on this journey. Each of the guides will leave you a gift. You can try to receive information from these gifts by either becoming the gift, and speaking as if you were the object, or by simply letting it talk to you. You can also ask yourself questions about the gift and see what answers pop into your mind. All techniques are good, so use whichever one works best for you.

There is also a segment of this meditation in which you will get in touch with your root emotion and inner characters. The more you can get into the scene and feel and express your emotions, the better. Really allow yourself to feel your rage, shame, hopelessness, despair, loneliness, fear, or hurt. Allow yourself to hate and blame and judge. These are powerful emotions that need to be expressed and dealt with, not suppressed. The scene I will describe to evoke these emotions is a heart-rending one of environmental destruction. It is important to really give yourself permission to feel with intensity and say everything you need to say. If the particular scene I am describing does not have an emotional impact for you, substitute another scene that does evoke your outrage and condemnation.

If you are taping this meditation yourself, don't forget to cue your subconscious during the induction by saying a couple of times that you are going to take the journey to the Beloved. Also, give yourself adequate time for your responses at the appropriate intervals during the meditation.

The Meditation

Sense yourself in your safe place, at just the right time of day. Imagine it or just pretend. See the colors first, the blues and greens and golds of a majestic Mother Earth. Wrap her in her colors warm and cool. See her with the eyes of love, all decked out in mystic hues of never-ending life: a riot of color, depth and dimension, a symphony of calling birds, flapping wings, whirring insects and whispering winds, a potpourri of fragrance, scents and smells to fill your nostrils and breathe deeply in.

Feel yourself standing, solid and grounded, in the midst of it all, as color and sound take shape to become the landscape all around. Look at the details now. See each blade of grass or each grain of sand as you feel the pebbles beneath your feet. Gaze with wonder at a leaf that is the home of an insect's eggs, or at a spider's web, or at the fluff of a dandelion blowing in the breeze. Feel the texture and temperature of rock or bark or water. Experience all there is for you to see and taste and touch, smell and hear. Give yourself permission to have the treasures of your safe place.

This earth is our Mother's vibrant jewel, her gift of tenderest love to you. Touch it, hold it, and place it in your heart. Feel the ache of love for the Mother's mountains, plains, and seas. Feel the laughter in the bubbling brooks, the singing of her birds, the rustling leaves, or the rhythmic crashing of her waves. Feel her majesty in each golden bar of light as it shimmers on the water or sparkles green and iridescent on each blade of grass, leaf, or tree. Let your safe place come alive with her love as you feel her heart beating underneath your feet.

And as you think these thoughts, you discover a path and find yourself wandering away, out of the safety, away from the love. You do not know why you go, you know only that you feel compelled to go and explore and discover all the many facets and dimensions of who you are.... Days pass, sunrises and sunsets without number. The moon grows full and wanes many times as the months cycle through the seasons.... The years come and go, but still you wander on, always searching, searching for that spark of who you are.

On and on you go until you come to a modern city and stand aghast, looking at the rows and rows of houses, factories, and shops. You sniff the air and smell the smog and see the trash piled high in dumps or in the streets. Your eyes burn, your nose recoils at the stench, and then you wander on, back into the peaceful wilderness. You are weary now. You have traveled a long, hard road. What was it all for, you wonder? What was it all for? You have gone so far from the safety. Where is your home? Where is your safe place where you are loved and cared for by unseen friends and nurtured and comforted by unseen hands? Where, oh where, in all this wide world, is your Beloved, who holds you safe and warm with an open heart in their loving arms?

As these fearful thoughts flow through your mind, you round another turn in the road and stop dead in your tracks. Your mouth drops open in dread and pain at the sight that meets your eyes. Your Mother Earth has been raped and ruined. The trees are gone, cut down into stumps. Slash and upheaval is everywhere. Devastation, ugliness, gaping holes, betrayal. No birds sing; there are no homes for animals or birds, no shelter from the sun or rain, nothing but miles and miles of hate and greed as far as the eye can see. The safety is gone, the grace and the love have been extinguished by the lumberjack's saw. Feel your feelings!

Your root emotion rises in your chest and comes to talk to you. Perhaps it is anger that you feel first, or loneliness, or fear. Perhaps hopelessness or shame or a terrible gnawing despair. Perhaps it is hurt you feel the most, an unendurable pain that begins to overwhelm you as you look about you at the desecration. You want to blame and blame and blame. Let it talk to you, your root emotion. Let it hate and hurt. Listen to what it has to say about what's become of this sacred land, this beautiful Mother Earth. (Silent taping for two minutes as you feel your feelings.)

Now, as you stand staring at this horror, a new thought comes to you and you remember what you came to the physical plane to learn: that you create your own reality and that, if this is true, you created this as well. No, not that you actually held the saw within your hands, but that you live in a consensus reality that allows it and therefore you are just as much at fault as anybody else. And then you remember also that what you see around you is just a reflection of all that you harbor within. Let the pain and fear and ugliness of that thought sink deeply in.

Now, let your root emotion turn itself on you and let your inner characters speak the words they have to say. Perhaps it is your judge or bully who comes forth to tell you you'd better do something about this mess, or who tells you how stupid you are to let it happen. Or maybe it's your victim who comes forth and feels their shame about being part of a human race that could do such a terrible thing. Maybe your rebel speaks up and says who gives a damn anyway, or maybe Mr. or Ms. Together looks at the devastation and says it will just grow back again and everything will be all right. Now let your root emotions talk to you through the voices of your inner characters and see what they have to say. (Silent taping for two minutes while you express your fear and pain.)

As your root emotion, spoken through the mouth of your inner characters, beats you, feel yourself giving way to the pain and fear. Feel your loneliness and despair. How can I ever heal this? This is too big for me, too much. I must run away and hide, but where? There is no safe place anywhere on our planet. It has all been raped and ruined by pollution. The human race has destroyed her with its greed. As the voice of fear slowly begins to tear you apart, paralyze you, numb you, you slowly sink into oblivion, totally exhausted, until you lie unconscious on the ground. No thought. No feeling. It has all been wrung out of you. No emotion, no love, no hate, nothing. Just let all sensation go as you disappear inside yourself and fall into a deep, deep sleep.

But as you sleep you begin to dream a happy dream. And in your dream, you seem to split in two. The part of you that is the voice of Love separates itself from the voice of fear and rises high above and hovers, watching the sleeping body it left behind.... Now, as you place your whole consciousness in the voice of Love, you look down on a sleeping body, numb with fear. A deep compassion wells up within you for the body lying there. Everything looks so different from this vantage point as you rise higher, and still higher, in the air.

The higher you climb, the lighter you become, until all at once you can see your Beloved, standing on a mountain top. You go to join them there. Looking into their eyes, you feel their love pour all through you like a molten flame of light. As they place their lips on yours, without fear, you surrender entirely to their love. Now that the voice of Love has been set free, your heart is full, open and ready to receive. Looking into their eyes, you say, "I knew that you would come, my Beloved, to hold me in your arms again and take me home to our safe place." And with a voice so pure it melts your heart, they reply, "I have always been here, my love, waiting for you to want to come home to me again."

You feel so full. Your cup of love is running over as you allow yourself to be surrounded by the vastness of their love. "I love you so," you tell them. "I will never let you go." And with eyes that are two deep pools of light, your Beloved looks into yours, smiles and replies, "I know, dear one. And I will never leave you either. For you are my heart and I am your soul, and with you, I will always go." As Heart looks into the depths of Soul to find itself, and as Soul comes to understand the longings of the Heart, your two sparks become as one and are wedded in a single flame of brilliant light.

But looking down, you see your body sound asleep, lying upon the ground. You know that the consciousness that is still within your body has not shared in your love today. And so, motioning to your Beloved to look, you say, "There seems to be a part of me that doubts. They are so lost and afraid, how can we teach them the truth? What can we do to heal them of their pain?" Your Beloved says, "I know — we'll send two guides to help them on their way. One will give them courage and one will make them meek. As they learn to listen to their words, we'll draw them up the path to us."

Now, placing your consciousness back in your body, you begin to stir and toss and turn a little.... Finally, you stretch and yawn and open your eyes.... Much to your surprise, you discover, standing before you, a new-born baby lamb, pure of heart and full of grace. Reaching out a hand, you place your fingers in the thick, soft wool and look into its little face. To your even greater surprise, the lamb begins to speak to you. Though its lips never move, you hear the words come into your mind. It tells you that it has come here to guide you home to your safe place. You wonder how such a meek, little creature could possibly know the way, but it tells you that size is not what counts. Love and willingness are what really matter. Then it tells you how you are like it, innocent in every way, just like everyone else, beyond blame and beyond punishment. How could anyone be blamed or punished for not knowing how to love, and even though you made mistakes, all is forgiven because that's what love is all about. It tells you, "As you walk with me, I will teach you to let go of the past and walk with love in eternal innocence as you let go of blame."

You are intrigued by this little one and what it has to say, but now it must go. As it turns and wanders off, it tells you that you will see it many times in the coming days, but for now, another guide will come to take its place. You are saddened but as it fades from view, you discover it has left you a gift for you to contemplate. You see it there on the ground. Go over and pick it up, become the gift and let it speak to you. It will tell you something about how to let go of judgment and go beyond blame. (Two minutes of silent taping while you discern its meaning.)

You look left and right, looking for your new guide. To your surprise you see an enormous lion, strong and brave. You don't know whether to run or just pray that it will disappear, but before you do either, it begins to talk to you. It tells you about your inner strength and how you have enough courage to face all your fears. It tells you about your personal power, which is the only real power, and how it can help you overcome any difficulty with determination and perseverance. It tells you that you are neither helpless nor alone, and that once you change your attitude, there is literally nothing that you cannot do.

At last it, too, tells you that it must go but that you will see it again, many times before the journey is done. And as it fades from view, it also leaves a gift to comfort you. Become the gift and let it speak. It will tell you something about your strength, courage, and your ability to persevere. (Two minutes silent taping while you discern the meaning of the symbol.)

Now, you rise from this desolate spot, and you know precisely what you are to do. You find a path and begin a climb that will take you to a mountain top. With your eyes focused on the heights, you travel for many days, and each time you come to a branching of the road, an inner voice always tells you precisely what to do and where to go. You have many dreams along the way. They are mostly happy dreams in which a guide comes to be with you. Sometimes the guide comes in the form of a lion and sometimes a lamb. But whichever form it is, it always points with certainty toward the promised land.

At last you make it to the top and, as you climb over the last precipice, the view that greets you is astonishing: brilliant blue skies free of smog and fumes, mountain lakes filled with pure water, rivers and streams that flow into a dazzling sea that sparkles under a radiant sun. The land has repaired itself and again is shelter for the creeping, crawling things, the winged ones, animals and plants without number.... But most surprising of all the things you see are a lion and lamb that laugh and play together....

With this vision held safe within your heart, you realize for the first time that it was your innocence that was your strength, because it gave you the courage to go beyond blame so that you could become responsible enough to change.

With the dawning of this revelation, you discover that there is someone else on this mountain top, for out of the shadows steps your Beloved, who has come to be with you. As your Beloved stands transfixed in wonder at the sight of you upon a mountain top, they look deep into your eyes and say with great emotion, "I knew that you would overcome your fear so that you could be with me again."

And you laugh and say, "Dear Beloved, didn't you know? There was no other way I could go. I had to come because I heard a voice calling me. It was the voice of Love, and it would not let me be."

Now, the voice of fear, which held within its darkness a tiny spark of light, united with the mighty voice of Love, which had heard fear's voice and cared enough to heal its fright. As the two voices become as one in you, your Beloved unites with you too. And in a blaze of glory, you and your Beloved, together, are lifted from the Earth and disappear into heaven's blissful home, forever and forever.

And in a moment you will open your eyes; your eyes will open at the count of five and not before. One, coming all the way back into your body. Two, beginning to sense your external environment. Three, wiggling fingers and toes. Four and five, open your eyes. Awake, alert, alive and refreshed.

Welcome back to Mother Earth.

The Mother's Mystery

My body is a temple glorious
    sanctified by holy love
The sacred is within me
    throbbing through my veins
I am the heart beat of heavenly grace
    a lustful desire for the great unknown
My womb of darkness is glorified
    by the radiant light of unearthly love.

NEW WORLD LIBRARY is dedicated to
publishing books and audiocassettes that help
improve the quality of our lives.

For a catalog of our fine books and cassettes, contact:

New World Library
14 Pamaron Way
Novato, California 94949
Phone: (415) 884-2100
Fax: (415) 884-2199

Or call toll free:
(800) 227-3900